People say that life is the thing, but I prefer reading.

Logan Pearsall Smith: *Afterthoughts* 1931

Contents

1• Personality

PRE-READING 1 **Complete the sentences with the key words in bold from the text.**

1 Researchers long ago found a _____ between cigarette smoking and lung cancer, but smoking is still quite popular despite these negative _____.

2 There is also some _____ that second-hand smoke, breathing in smoke from other people's cigarettes, can be harmful as well.

3 Though the film was popular, _____ complained that it was just another predictable and unrealistic action film.

4 She made several _____ about the future, but none of them were _____.

PRE-READING 2 **Read the text below and answer the question.**

> ### Hard-working employees wanted: Libras and Virgos need not apply
>
> In 2009, an insurance company in Austria ran a job advertisement in several major newspapers that read, 'We are looking for people over 20 for part-time jobs in sales and management with the following star signs: Capricorn, Taurus, Aquarius, Aries and Leo.' Several equality groups complained that this was not a fair employment practice.

What do you think about this kind of employment practice?

 a Astrology is fairly accurate, so it is OK for the company to do this.

 b Astrology might be accurate in some cases, but not for everyone. It is rather unfair for the company to do this.

 c Astrology is not accurate. This is a very unfair practice.

Discuss your answer with a partner.

As above, so below?

In 1979 a French researcher, Michel Gauquelin, took out an advertisement in a Paris newspaper offering free personalized horoscopes. To the first 150 people who responded, he sent out readings giving details of their personality, and then he asked them to report back on the accuracy of the information. An amazing 94 per cent replied that their readings were very **accurate**. There were two things the researcher did not mention to the respondents, however. Firstly, all 150 people, regardless of their actual birthdates, received the same reading, word for word. Secondly, the reading that they received was one prepared with the time and date of birth of a French doctor called Michel Petiot, who was convicted of multiple murders during the Second World War.

Astrology is the belief that the position of planets and stars at the time of a person's birth has a strong influence on the person's character and future. Astrology originated in ancient Babylonia more than 3,000 years ago, and is still believed by a sizable percentage of people in the West. Recent surveys have found that 31 per cent of Americans believe in astrology, and 52 per cent of Europeans consider astrology to be a science. Many newspapers in the West carry horoscopes, allowing people to get daily advice according to the astrological sign corresponding to their particular birthdate. Astrology is not just for the average person, either. Former US President Ronald Reagan was a believer in astrology, and according to a presidential aide, every major decision taken by the President during his eight years in office was first checked with a well-known astrologer. Former French President Jacques Chirac is said to have checked his horoscope every morning.

Despite the popularity of astrology, the scientific community questions the accuracy of this theory. For example, another study by Michel Gauquelin examined the horoscopes of 15,560 professionals from five European countries, and could find no **link** between astrological signs and occupations. Perhaps the most damaging studies have been the ones on *astro-twins* (here defined as people who are born on the same day). The premise is simple: if one's date of birth has an effect on one's character and future, then people born on the same day should be more similar to each other than to those born on different days. These studies examined thousands of people who shared birthdates, looking for similarities in personality and intelligence, yet found that these people had no more in common with their astro-twin than with anyone else. Scientists also say that a belief in astrology has potential for confirming stereotypes and encouraging discrimination.

If researchers largely dismiss astrology as superstition, why do so many people in the West still believe it? For most, it is based on their personal experience. They have found it works for them, so what does it matter what the studies say? **Critics** of astrology, however, counter this 'but it works for me' defence with two explanations regarding why beliefs in astrology may seem justified to some. The first is called confirmation bias. Confirmation bias refers to the tendency of people to pay more attention to evidence which seems to agree with and justify their beliefs, and to ignore or forget any **evidence** that suggests they might be wrong. Someone might remember a particular time, for example, when an astrologer told them they would find love in a particular year, but forget the other times when the astrologer got their **predictions** wrong.

Secondly, there is what is known as the Forer effect. The Forer effect states that people tend to view general statements that could apply to many people as being highly accurate for them individually. Consider the following statements: How many are true for you?
- You seem calm and in control on the outside, but on in the inside you sometimes feel uncertain and afraid.
- You are an independent thinker, and accept new ideas only after careful evaluation.
- At times you are shy, but in some circumstances you can be outgoing and talkative.

Do most of those descriptions match you? Well, it turns out that the majority of people find those statements **true** for them (only a very few people are shy in *all* situations, for example). This explains why nearly all the people who replied to Gauquelin's advertisement thought the horoscope reading matched them well individually.

Regardless of whether or not there is any truth in astrology, for many people it is something they do for fun and don't take very seriously. Annie, an American university student, says 'I really don't know if astrology is true or not, but it's something fun to talk about with friends, and it's always interesting to read my horoscope in the morning and see if it turns out right. As long as I'm not paying money to let an astrologer tell me how to run my life, what's the harm?'

COMPREHENSION 1 **Decide if the sentences are True (T) or False (F). Then write the line number where the evidence is.**

1 The research reported in the first paragraph gives evidence of the accuracy of astrology.

T ☐   F ☐   Line number: _____

2 Astrology is believed by millions of people in America and Europe.

T ☐   F ☐   Line number: _____

3 Most scientific research does not support astrology.

T ☐   F ☐   Line number: _____

4 Confirmation bias can mean remembering only evidence that supports your beliefs, and forgetting evidence that goes against your beliefs.

T ☐   F ☐   Line number: _____

5 The Forer effect shows that quite often, astrologers can give exact and highly accurate information about people.

T ☐   F ☐   Line number: _____

6 The article suggests that many people who believe in astrology are not harmed by it.

T ☐   F ☐   Line number: _____

COMPREHENSION 2 **Answer the questions.**

1 In line 9, what does the expression *word for word* mean?

a Using different words, but having the same meaning

b Using exactly the same words

c Using the same number of words

2 In line 28, what does the phrase, *questions the accuracy of this theory* mean?

a They don't understand why the theory is accurate

b They are very curious about the accuracy of the theory

c They have strong doubts about the accuracy of the theory

3 In line 33, what does *premise* mean?

a A statement on which a theory can be based

b A solution to a question

c An idea which is false

4 In line 42, *largely* means …

a mostly   b in a big way   c strongly   d loudly

5   What is the meaning of lines 67-68?

   a   You feel calm when you are in natural places, like parks and mountains, but feel nervous and afraid inside buildings

   b   You are calm in familiar places, but can feel afraid in new or strange places

   c   Even though you might feel upset or scared, you appear calm to other people

6   In the final paragraph, what word or expression means *happens in a particular way*?

     _____

SPEAKING

Discuss the questions with a partner.

1   What is your star sign? Do you consider it an accurate description of your personality?

2   Most scientists reject astrology. What is your reaction to this?

   a   They are probably right. It is just a superstition.

   b   They might be wrong. Perhaps more research is necessary.

   c   They are probably wrong. It seems clear that there is a link between one's star sign and personality.

3.   What other beliefs do you know which claim to predict people's personalities? Do you think they are accurate?

VOCABULARY FOCUS 1

Complete the sentences with the correct word.

For example:

Who knows what will happen next year? No one can _predict_ the future!

   a   prove   **b**   ~~predict~~   **c**   reject   **d**   justify

1   In the West, there is a _____ that breaking a mirror brings bad luck. No one really believes it these days, though.

   a   superstition   **b**   theory   **c**   warning   **d**   stereotype

2   Saying you cheated in a test because your mark is important to you is not a good reason for cheating. There is no good excuse you can make to _____ cheating.

   a   prove   **b**   deny   **c**   state   **d**   justify

3   The company only employs white people, so some people are accusing it of racial _____.

   a   discrimination   **b**   conformity   **c**   influence   **d**   warning

4 The researcher wants to test her new _____ about language learning. She's not sure if it will work, but she wants to find out.

   a candidate **b** stereotype **c** theory **d** survey

5 Although some people smoke and never fall ill, the _____ for becoming ill is much higher in people who smoke.

   a warning **b** accuracy **c** potential **d** trend

6 This new product is not safe. We need to _____ people not to buy it.

   a justify **b** deny **c** conclude **d** warn

7 I'm a bit of a _____ of the new government. I don't think it does anything right.

   a critic **b** researcher **c** broadcaster **d** psychologist

8 Why do you think that all European men smoke and drink too much? That's just a _____. There are many who do not.

   a theory **b** superstition **c** stereotype **d** trend

VOCABULARY FOCUS 2

Circle all the words that match your personality.

Aries:	passionate, direct, **creative**
Taurus:	calm, peaceful, stable
Gemini:	adaptable, clever, active
Cancer:	loving, dependable, helpful, cautious
Leo:	**confident**, **outgoing**, proud, trusting
Virgo:	perfectionist, hard-working, **selfish**
Libra	fair, sociable, **friendly**, romantic
Scorpio:	mysterious, powerful, charismatic
Sagittarius:	enthusiastic, adventurous, **optimistic**
Capricorn:	ambitious, patient, **proud**, **stubborn**
Aquarius:	**independent**, individualistic, **considerate**
Pisces:	spiritual, sensitive, idealistic, creative

In the text on page 11, several words are in **bold**. Write them next to the correct antonym below.

For example: lazy _hard-working_

1	dependent	_____	**6**	shy	_____
2	pessimistic	_____	**7**	insecure	_____
3	unoriginal	_____	**8**	selfish	_____
4	adaptable	_____	**9**	cold	_____
5	considerate	_____	**10**	humble	_____

Grammar	We often shorten relative clauses. The relative pronouns *that* and *who*, and the following *be* verb, are optional in these sentences:
Relative clauses	Beliefs **that are** based on superstition … → Beliefs based on superstition …
	A broadcaster **who is** named Naomi … → A broadcaster named Naomi …
	Americans **that are** aged between 13 and 64 … → Americans aged between 13 and 64 …

GRAMMAR 1   **Read the sentences and cross out the unnecessary words.**

For example:

This theory is based on studies ~~that were~~ conducted in 2001.

1   Students who are coming early tomorrow will get extra points.

2   The lady who is working on the contract said she hasn't finished.

3   The man brought in a bag that was full of money.

4   Actors who are in blockbusters often become very famous.

GRAMMAR 2   **Combine the sentences into one using relative clauses. Then reduce the relative clause.**

For example:

I have a friend. He is living abroad. He speaks English well.

I have a friend living abroad who speaks English well.

1   My friend has a book. The book was signed by Stephen King.

2   Islam is a religion. The religion was founded by the Prophet Muhammad.

3   *The Lord of the Rings* is a film. The film was based on a book.

4   The pyramids in Egypt are huge structures. They were built by thousands of slaves.

Effective • *Skills*

Read the following passage and indicate how closely each personality type is like you.

Are blood group and personality related?

In the West, some people believe that an individual's personality and character can be predicted according to the time of the year that the person was born. The Chinese believe that the year of birth determines character. In the past century, a relatively new belief has arisen: the idea that personality is related to ABO blood group. The blood-group personality theory started in Japan in 1927, when a secondary-school administrator noticed personality similarities and differences among his staff. The theory soon went out of fashion, but was brought back in force in the 1970s. The belief is still strong in Japan, and is now becoming increasingly popular in neighbouring countries.

Is the belief accurate, or is it just a modern-day superstition? Why not test it for yourself? First read each description and decide how well it matches your own personality. Then check to see if the ABO blood-group theory accurately predicted your personality.

1   People with this blood group are individualistic. They are creative and curious, and are always open to new adventures and challenges. They live life with passion, and tend to be optimistic and outgoing. Their main weakness is a tendency to be selfish, which can cause them to be irresponsible and forgetful of others. They are unpredictable, which can make them very entertaining and charming, but this can also make close relationships with them difficult. They can also be jealous. They are often good cooks.

___ This is me exactly
___ This is generally like me
___ Some things are like me, but not all of them
___ This isn't generally like me
___ I'm completely different

2 People with this blood group are natural leaders. They are confident, charismatic and ambitious, and prefer to be the centre of attention. Even in defeat they are optimistic about the future. They are often athletic and prefer to be active. Their main weakness is pride, which can lead them to be stubborn. They love to be around people, but also tend to be uncommitted in relationships. They often have trouble finishing what they start.

__ This is me exactly

__ This is generally like me

__ Some things are like me, but not all of them

__ This isn't generally like me

__ I'm completely different

3 People with this blood group are serious and hard-working. They are generally conservative, responsible and tend to follow the rules. They are often perfectionists, wanting everything to be done properly, and they feel stressed when things don't work out the way they planned. They seem calm and focused in difficult situations, but they tend to avoid confrontations and arguments. They are usually shy and quiet, and can be sensitive to criticism. They tend to be cautious, and can be very stubborn about doing what they feel is right. They are well-organized and punctual. They make keen gardeners.

__ This is me exactly

__ This is generally like me

__ Some things are like me, but not all of them

__ This isn't generally like me

__ I'm completely different

4 People with this blood group are contradictory, easily switching from one extreme to another. They can be cool and confident one moment, then sensitive and indecisive the next. They can be outgoing and sociable in some situations, but then shy at other times. They are very considerate and generous to some people, but also strict, critical, and unforgiving to others. Generally, they are unpredictable and independent, seeing themselves as separate from the group. They are often very analytical and rational in their views.

__ This is me exactly

__ This is generally like me

__ Some things are like me, but not all of them

__ This isn't generally like me

__ I'm completely different

DISCUSSION   **Complete the sentences with information about you.**

1   The personality I am most like is number __.

2   Other personalities that are similar to me are numbers __.

3   The personality that is unlike me is number __.

What is your blood group? Check below to see which descriptions match the blood groups. Did the ABO blood-group personality theory accurately predict your personality? Discuss the answer with a partner.

> 1.   =   blood group B
> 2.   =   blood group O
> 3.   =   blood group A
> 4.   =   blood group AB

a   It was very accurate. The description of my blood group is more accurate for me than any other.

b   It was fairly accurate. The description of my blood group matches me well, but so does the description of another blood group.

c   It wasn't very accurate. Other blood-group descriptions match me more closely.

d   It was mostly wrong.

e   It was completely wrong!

SUMMARY CORRECTION   **The following summary has incorrect information in each sentence. <u>Underline</u> the mistakes.**

The ABO blood-group personality theory claims that our blood group can shape our future. It was first proposed by a scientist in Japan in the 1920s. It became largely forgotten for several decades, but then became popular again beginning in the 1990s. People in blood group A are considered to be hard workers and somewhat liberal. Type A people are hard-working perfectionists who enjoy confrontation. They tend to be disorganized, sensitive and punctual.

People in blood group B tend to be very creative and considerate. They love challenges and easily make close relationships. People in blood group O like to set big goals for their future, and usually finish what they start. They enjoy meeting their friends and new people, and are unlikely to divorce. Finally, people in the AB blood group are not always good at following rules, but they are always sociable. Their personality doesn't change often, and generally they are very logical in their views.

2•Punishment

Complete the sentences with the key words in bold from the text.

1 The teacher found out that Alan had cheated in the test. As
_____, she gave him a grade F.

2 Whenever I did something wrong when I was a child, my father
would give me a _____ for at least 30 minutes about it.

3 Before CDs and MP3 players, many people would buy music on a
_____.

4 At the shop, Julie decided to _____ some sweets because
she wanted some, but didn't have any money.

Discuss the questions with a partner.

1 When you were younger and you did something wrong, how did
your parents usually punish you?

   a They would make me do some work.
   b They would not allow me to do something.
   c They would smack or hit me.
   d They would just give me a lecture.

2 Did the punishment make you improve, or did you make the same
mistakes again?

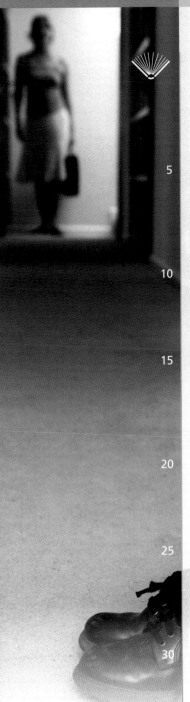

An unpunished crime

The first time I got caught stealing was when I was about eight years old. My mother, older brother, and I went shopping at a department store. While my mother and brother were looking at clothes, I went alone to the music department. I noticed a Michael Jackson **cassette**
5 and, without really thinking, put it in my pocket. Then I went back to my mother and brother, and continued shopping.

Later, while we were driving home in the car, I decided to look at my new cassette. My brother saw it and asked me where I had bought it. I was unable to answer, and my brother immediately told my mother
10 that I had stolen the cassette. As soon as my mother found out what I had done, she turned the car round and we went back to the department store. She dragged me into the shop by my ear, and made me return the cassette and apologize. It was extremely embarrassing. It didn't end there. My mother told my father and he
15 shouted at me for what seemed like forever. As a **punishment**, I couldn't see my friends for the rest of the summer holiday (two whole weeks!). The experience made me very angry, but I did learn two things that day: one, when you do something wrong, be very careful not to get caught, and two, never trust your brother.

20 A few years later, at middle school, I made a new friend, Andy, who was a bad influence on me. Andy never went to school and was always getting in trouble. I thought Andy was cool and I wanted to impress him. When I found out that he often liked to **shoplift**, I felt that I had to do it, too, to show that I was just as cool. Every day after
25 school, we would go to shops and steal sweets, cassettes, cards, cigarettes, and anything else that we could lay our hands on. Andy liked to call it 'shopping with a five-finger discount.'

One day, Andy and I were shoplifting in a supermarket, when suddenly a shop assistant grabbed me. She saw me putting a cassette
30 in my pocket (I had bad luck with cassettes). As soon as Andy saw that I was caught, he quickly left the store. I don't blame him, as there was nothing he could do to help me. The police arrived and took me home in a police car. I was terrified. The police officer talked with my mother and then left. I expected my mother to be furious,
35 just as she had been before, and was waiting for the severe punishment that was sure to come. However, to my surprise, she just broke down and cried. For a long 20 minutes, my mother just wept. I pleaded with her to stop crying and I promised I would never steal again, but she wouldn't stop. I had not only let her down, but I had
40 broken her heart. I felt terrible to see her so upset. She didn't go on at me or punish me at all. She didn't even give me a **lecture** about stealing, or tell my father.

45

50

After that day, I refused to steal again and I never have since. Even today, when I think about stealing, I get that same sick feeling in my stomach and heart that I had the day my mother cried in front of me. Why that 'non-punishment' was so much more effective than the 'real' punishment I received when I was eight years old, I am not sure, but it makes me think about how I will punish and discipline my daughter when she does something bad. I learnt something else from that experience, as well. When I told Andy that I wouldn't shoplift again, he was fine about it and we continued to be friends as before. I realized then that a true friend never pressures you to do something bad, and accepts you for who you are.

COMPREHENSION 1   **Complete the table with short answers.**

	What did he steal?	How was he caught?	What did his parents do?	What was the result?
First time stealing				
Last time stealing				

COMPREHENSION 2   **Answer the questions.**

1   What did the author learn from his first experience with stealing?

    a   Stealing is wrong.

    b   His older brother really loves him.

    c   Be more careful not to get caught.

2   Why did the author decide to steal when he was at middle school?

    a   He didn't have any money.

    b   He wanted his friend to like him.

    c   He didn't think he would get caught.

3   Why did the author decide never to steal again?

    a   He was afraid of getting caught again.

    b   He realized that it was not a good thing to do.

    c   His friend didn't want him to steal anymore.

4   What did the author find out about Andy?

    a   Andy would still be his friend even if he didn't steal.

    b   Andy didn't want to steal again either.

    c   Andy was not really a true friend.

COMPREHENSION 3   **Answer the questions.**

1   In line 9, what does the author mean when he says, *I was unable to answer?*
   a   He didn't know the answer.
   b   He couldn't understand the question.
   c   He didn't want to tell the truth.

2   In line 14, what does *It* in *It didn't end there* refer to?
   a   his general punishment
   b   his mother's anger
   c   his embarrassment at the department store

3   In line 24, what does *cool* mean?
   a   quite cold
   b   good
   c   stupid

4   In line 26, what does *anything … we could lay our hands on* mean?
   a   They stole anything that it was possible to steal.
   b   They stole anything that they could hide in their hands.
   c   They stole anything that was easy to reach.

5   In line 31, what does the author mean when he says about Andy, *I don't blame him?*
   a   Andy was not wrong to steal.
   b   It was OK for Andy to leave the store without helping the author.
   c   The author did not get caught because of Andy.

6   In line 37, what does *broke down* mean?
   a   to not function properly
   b   to fall down
   c   to lose control of one's emotions

7   In line 41, which expression means *to criticize someone because they did something wrong?* _____

8   In lines 52–53, what does *a true friend … accepts you for who you are* mean?
   a   A good friend will like you if you are the right kind of person.
   b   A good friend should try to understand exactly who you are.
   c   You don't have to change yourself or do something special for a friend to like you.

SPEAKING **Discuss the questions with a partner.**

1 Do you agree with the punishment the author received when he was eight years old? What would your parents do in a similar situation? What would you do if you were the parent?

2 When the author was caught stealing at the supermarket, what did his friend Andy do? What do you think about Andy's action? What would you have done if you were Andy?

VOCABULARY <u>Underline</u> **the word that does not belong in each group.**
FOCUS 1

For example:

nice	pleasant	<u>terrible</u>	fantastic
1 normal	typical	extreme	average
2 severe	weak	mild	soft
3 influence	criticize	discourage	complain
4 rules	discipline	punishment	freedom

VOCABULARY **Complete the sentences with the correct word.**
FOCUS 2

1 I hate shopping, but my girlfriend _____ me to the shopping centre anyway.

    a influenced **b** dragged **c** embarrassed **d** grabbed

rules

severe   *complain*

2 I was so _____ when I fell over in the bus. Everyone laughed!

    a intrigued **b** apologized **c** blamed **d** embarrassed

3 Ken really _____ his parents when he failed three exams in his first term at university.

    a impressed **b** let down **c** influenced **d** broke down

4 When someone broke the window, the teacher _____ Paulo. But then she found out that someone else did it.

    a impressed **b** broke down **c** distressed **d** blamed

5 I felt really bad about getting angry for no reason with my friend, so I called and _____. Now everything is OK.

    a apologized **b** let him down **c** blamed him
    d went on at him

6 Linda got bad marks last term, so her father _____ her by taking away her mobile phone for one month. Ouch!

    a grabbed **b** punished **c** embarrassed **d** dragged

Grammar

Past progressive and past simple

Sentences with two past simple clauses indicate that one event happened after another (possibly as a result of the first action).

*When my mother **found out**, she **dragged** me back to the shop.*

In a sentence with a past simple clause and a past progressive clause, the past progressive clause indicates the activity that was already in progress. The past simple clause tells us what interrupted the activity that was in progress.

*One day, Andy and I **were shoplifting** in a supermarket, when suddenly a shop assistant **grabbed** me.*

Already in progress: *Andy and I **were shoplifting***

Event that occurred during this time: *suddenly a shop assistant **grabbed** me.*

GRAMMAR   **Answer the questions.**

1   Which sentence (**a** or **b**) is more logical?

   a   I was sleeping when the thief entered my house.

   b   I slept when the thief entered my house.

2   In which sentence is the subject afraid of the dog?

   a   He was running when he saw the dog.

   b   He ran when he saw the dog.

3   Which of the following situations is more likely?

   a   The pupil smoked a cigarette at school when the teacher appeared.

   b   The pupil was smoking a cigarette at school when the teacher appeared.

4   In which sentence is Alex embarrassed?

   a   The students were laughing when Alex came into the room.

   b   The students laughed when Alex came into the room.

5   Which sentence would be most upsetting for the speaker?

   a   She laughed when I told her I loved her.

   b   She was laughing when I told her I loved her.

6   Which sentence is more logical?

   a   He skied when he broke his leg.

   b   He was skiing when he broke his leg.

Effective • *Skills*

Here are some tips to increase your reading speed.

- Find a reading speed that pushes you to read a *little* faster than usual, but still allows you to understand well.

- Do not mouth the words (quietly say the words) as you read. This slows down your reading speed.

- Avoid re-reading phrases or sentences unless you really need to. Try to keep your eyes going forward.

- Concentrate! Keep your mind on understanding the reading and nothing else.

Use the tips to read the text. Record your start time before you begin reading.

Start **time:** _____

The Death of
IKEMEFUNA

This story is from the graded reader 'Things Fall Apart' by Chinua Achebe. It is about the life of Okonkwo, an African villager. A man from a nearby village accidentally killed someone in Okonkwo's village. As punishment, the nearby village had to send a young man, Ikemefuna, to live in Okonkwo's village.

Ikemefuna lived with Okonkwo for several years, and they loved each other like father and son. However, finally the village leaders decided that Ikemefuna must be killed as punishment for his village's crime. In this part of the story, the men take Ikemefuna out to the forest to kill him. Ikemefuna does not know what is going to happen.

The next day, the men returned to Okonkwo's house. They had a big pot of wine with them. They wore their best clothes. They looked as if they were going to a big meeting of the clan, or on a visit to another village. These men had bags over their shoulders and they carried machetes.
5 Okonkwo got ready quickly. They all left the compound and Ikemefuna carried the pot of wine on his head.

At first, all the men were talking and laughing. But the further they went, the quieter they became. The sun got hotter and the birds in the forest began to sing. The only noise was the birds singing and the sound of men's footsteps on the ground. Everybody was silent. Ikemefuna wondered why nobody was talking and he felt rather afraid.

10

Machete

The footpath got very narrow. They were right in the middle of the forest. The trees were getting bigger and taller. Some were covered with climbing plants. It looked as if nobody had been in the forest for years and years. The sun shone through the leaves and the trees, and made patterns of light and shade on the ground.

15

Ikemefuna heard a man whispering behind him. He turned round to see who it was. The man was telling the people to hurry up.

'We still have a long way to go,' the man said, 'so we must hurry.'

20 Then this man and another one went to the front and started walking more quickly. Everyone then walked more quickly. Ikemefuna was in the middle of them all. The men were still carrying their machetes and Ikemefuna still had the pot of wine on his head.

At first, Ikemefuna had been frightened. But he was not frightened any
25 more because Okonkwo was walking right behind him. Ikemefuna felt safe. Okonkwo was like a real father to him. Ikemefuna had never liked his own father and he had forgotten him after three years. But he loved Okonkwo.

Suddenly, one of the men walking behind Ikemefuna made a noise in his throat. Ikemefuna looked round and the man told him to walk on and not to
30 look back. He spoke in a frightening voice. His voice made Ikemefuna's whole body go very cold. Ikemefuna became frightened. His hands shook a little as they held the pot of wine.

Ikemefuna looked back again quickly. Okonkwo was not walking behind him now. He was right at the back of the line of men.

35 Ikemefuna's legs began to shake. He was afraid to look back again. The man behind him raised his machete quietly and quickly, and brought it down on Ikemefuna's head. Okonkwo heard the machete hit the pot of wine. The pot fell off Ikemefuna's head and broke on the ground. Okonkwo heard Ikemefuna cry out.

40 'My father, they have killed me,' Ikemefuna cried.

Ikemefuna ran towards Okonkwo. Okonkwo was very afraid, but he raised his own machete and brought it down onto Ikemefuna's head and killed him. Okonkwo did not want to do this. He was very afraid. And he loved Ikemefuna.
45 But he was afraid that his friends would think he was weak if he did not kill Ikemefuna.

Finish time: _____

COMPREHENSION   **Decide if the sentences are True (T) or False (F). Do not look back at the text.**

1   Ikemefuna carried a pot of wine on his head.   T ☐   F ☐

2   At first the men talked a lot, but later they became quiet.   T ☐   F ☐

3   Ikemefuna loved Okonkwo more than his real father.   T ☐   F ☐

4   Ikemefuna felt afraid because Okonkwo was walking directly behind him.   T ☐   F ☐

5   Before he was attacked, Ikemefuna seemed to have no idea that he was in danger.   T ☐   F ☐

6   Okonkwo was the first to attack Ikemefuna.   T ☐   F ☐

7   Ikemefuna tried to run away from Okonkwo.   T ☐   F ☐

8   In the end, Ikemefuna attacked Okonkwo.   T ☐   F ☐

9   Okonkwo did not want to kill Ikemefuna.   T ☐   F ☐

10   Okonkwo killed Ikemefuna because he was afraid of him.   T ☐   F ☐

SUMMARY COMPLETION   **Complete the text with the words in the box.**

killed   punishment   cried   frightened   weak
pot   shake   quiet   forest   laughing

Ikemefuna came to Okonkwo's village as (**1**)_____ for an accidental death. Ikemefuna lived with Okonkwo and they were happy together. However, the village leaders decided that Ikemefuna should be (**2**)_____. The village men took him to the (**3**)_____. They made him carry a (**4**)_____ of wine on his head. At first, they were talking and (**5**)_____, but later they become very (**6**)_____. Ikemefuna felt very (**7**)_____ and his legs began to (**8**)_____. Then, a man struck Ikemefuna on his head with a knife. Ikemefuna (**9**)_____ out to Okonkwo and ran towards him for help. Okonkwo was afraid that the other men would think he was (**10**)_____, so Okonkwo killed Ikemefuna.

Read the text and answer the questions in Exercise 2 as quickly as you can. Write your starting and finishing time.

Start time: _____

Finish time: _____

The body of superstitions

Perhaps all cultures in the world have superstitions relating physical features of the body to personality traits. England is no exception, and had a large number of such beliefs in the past. People with red hair, for example, were believed to be naturally hot-tempered. Black or dark brown hair was believed to indicate strength of character, while light-coloured hair implied the opposite. The shape of one's ears and nose were also said to be indicative of personality and character. Small ears indicated a gentle, delicate character, while people with thick, large ears were believed to be of a rougher nature. People with prominent noses were expected to be intelligent and determined, while those with thin noses were believed to be jealous and uncertain. Few people these days are even aware of these old superstitions, let alone claim to believe them. Yet some experts say that subconsciously, many of these beliefs might still exist.

EXERCISE 2

Decide if the sentences are True (T), False (F), or if the information is Not Given (NG) in the text.

1 The purpose of the text is to discuss old beliefs about personality in England.

   T ☐ F ☐ NG ☐

2 England has more superstitions about the body than other cultures.

   T ☐ F ☐ NG ☐

3 In the past, people believed that a person's personality had an effect on his/her body.

   T ☐ F ☐ NG ☐

4 According to the text, having black hair and a big nose is not desirable.

   T ☐ F ☐ NG ☐

5 People with fair hair were believed to have weak characters.

   T ☐ F ☐ NG ☐

6 Some people try to change their body because of these beliefs.

   T ☐ F ☐ NG ☐

EXERCISE 3

Complete the sentences with the words in the box. Use each word only once.

> analytical   enthusiastic   cautious
> loyal   charismatic   stubborn

1 A good prime minister should be _____. People who do not like their leaders usually do not follow them.

2 Many people have lost a lot of money investing in stocks and shares. They should have been more _____.

3 We explained why his plan doesn't work, but he is very _____ and won't change his mind.

4 Today, it seems that very few workers are _____ to their company. If another company offers them more money, they are quick to leave.

5 Students tend to be more _____ about subjects that they can relate to their own lives.

6 A good scientist is _____ and enjoys trying to find answers to problems.

EXERCISE 1

Read the text.

Creating an environment in which students feel accepted, secure, and free to explore is crucial to learning, but classroom discipline issues also need to be addressed. The teacher needs to create clear boundaries for permissible behaviour, while maintaining a relaxed, open environment for learning to take place. Teachers with easy-going personalities are often good at creating a positive learning environment, but if they are too **lenient** there may be major discipline problems. Young students are always trying to see how much they can get away with, and a teacher who is too friendly and **accommodating** will soon find that the class is completely out of control. Teachers with **strict** personalities and teaching styles usually have better classroom discipline, but going too far with rules can have a negative effect. When students make mistakes, which they inevitably will, strict reactions following the letter of the law may create a tense atmosphere which **inhibits** participation, especially if the teacher embarrasses the student in front of his or her peers.

EXERCISE 2

Answer the questions.

1   Which of the titles is most appropriate for the text?

   a   Developing a peaceful environment in the classroom

   b   The importance of making fair rules in the classroom

   c   Techniques for maintaining good classroom discipline

2   What type of teacher is not discussed in the text?

   a   Teachers who do not enforce strict rules.

   b   Teachers who expect students to follow their rules exactly.

   c   Teachers who demand a lot of homework.

3   What advice can be inferred from the text?

   a   If a teacher creates a positive learning environment, students will be less likely to break the rules.

   b   A good way to make the rules clear is to punish students in front of the class.

   c   Teachers should be consistent with rules.

EXERCISE 3

Match the keywords in bold from the text to the correct definitions (1–4).

1   Helpful and easy to work with

   _____

2   To make someone too embarrassed to behave in a normal way

   _____

3   Punishing someone less severely than they deserve

   _____

4   Expecting someone to obey the rules completely

   _____

3 • Extensive reading

PRE-READING 1 **Discuss these questions with a partner. Do you often read in English for private study?**

- If yes, what kind of reading do you do?

    a reading on the Internet
    b newspapers or magazines
    c books (for example Harry Potter books)
    d reading from English study books
    e other

- If no, what are the reasons why you do not read in English?

    a It's hard to find enjoyable material.
    b It's too slow and difficult to read in English.
    c I don't enjoy reading in general.
    d I don't have time.
    e I don't think it is necessary.

PRE-READING 2 **In your opinion, how useful is reading alone in developing the following language skills? Discuss your answers with a partner.**

Reading skills	very useful	quite useful	not useful
Writing skills	very useful	quite useful	not useful
Vocabulary	very useful	quite useful	not useful
Grammar	very useful	quite useful	not useful
Speaking skills	very useful	quite useful	not useful
Listening skills	very useful	quite useful	not useful

Simply read

In the mid-nineties, two language researchers conducted an interesting experiment with a group of students learning English at university. These students were retaking compulsory English courses they had previously failed. In language tests, these students were far behind the other university students. As most of these students disliked studying English, few expected any improvement.

The researchers put these students in a special class for the second term of their English course. The class met for the same amount of time as the other English courses, but the teaching was very different. At the end of the term, the students took another language test and the results were surprising. In just one term, the students in the special class improved so much that their results in the new tests were almost as good as those of the other students. Not only had their English improved greatly, but many of these students, who used to dread English, now enjoyed the class.

Extensive reading

What was the 'secret method' that produced such dramatic results in these previously reluctant learners? The class was an extensive reading course. Extensive reading is simply reading a lot of English (reading almost every day) at a fairly easy level (being able to understand the text without needing a dictionary). The students on the above-mentioned course spent almost all of their class time simply reading enjoyable books.

In study after study, researchers have found that extensive reading can play a big part in successful language learning. In fact, one study investigating language-learning strategies found that reading for pleasure and looking for opportunities to read in English were the two factors most closely related to successful language learning.

Reading and writing

It should come as no surprise that extensive reading helps students improve reading skills. Several studies have shown that students doing extensive reading for more than one year are almost always better readers than students who have only done the usual readings in class Extensive reading also allows students to improve their reading speed more quickly than just by reading difficult texts. In short, people can learn to read well simply by reading a lot, at an appropriate level.

What is even more surprising is how much extensive reading improves students' writing skills. In one study, students on extensive reading programmes were evaluated as being 2–3 times better at writing compared with students who did not read much, yet actually practised writing more! Many other researchers have come to similar conclusions. Students who just read a lot can make equal or greater progress in writing than students who actually practise writing, at least where beginner and intermediate students are concerned. This does not mean that practising writing is unnecessary! Writing practice and extensive reading can be a powerful combination in developing writing skills.

Extensive reading and speaking skills

Not only can extensive reading benefit reading and writing skills; it can also develop speaking and listening skills, though to a lesser extent. One study of learning strategies found that reading outside the classroom was the most significant influence on oral communicative ability. Students who read a lot are more likely to speak well. Other researchers have found that students just reading graded readers (simplified books especially for language students) improved in both fluency and accuracy of expression in their speaking, even though they did very little speaking during the course of the study.

TOEFL tests

Do you want to have a good score in a test like TOEFL? Perhaps you should start thinking about extensive reading. Researchers have found that students who often read in English in their free time tend to have high TOEFL scores, while those who do not tend to have low scores. They found that reading was a better predictor of TOEFL performance than the number of years spent studying English or living in English-speaking countries. Another study showed that students who only read enjoyable books consistently improved their TOEFL scores, averaging 3–4 points in the test each week of reading.

How is it that just reading can bring all these benefits? Extensive reading allows students to language in context over and over again, giving them the exposure they need to understand, organize, remember, and use it. Extensive reading also gives repetition of key vocabulary and grammar items, both essential to successful language learning. In short, extensive reading provides a very strong foundation on which to build language skills.

Extensive reading is not the only way to learn a language. Most language experts would agree that language students still need to spend a lot of time practising speaking, listening, writing, and so on, in order to become proficient in a language. However, including extensive reading in your private study can certainly do great things for your language ability. Not only is extensive reading effective, but it can be a very enjoyable way to learn a new language as well. Give it a try and see what it can do for you!

COMPREHENSION 1   **Decide if the sentences are True (T) or False (F). Then write the line number where the evidence is.**

1   In paragraph 1, the students chosen for the study were those who had failed previous English courses and did not like English classes.

T ☐   F ☐   Line number: _____

2   After the experiment, the students in the extensive reading class did better in tests than students in the normal English classes.

T ☐   F ☐   Line number: _____

3   We can infer that most of the students in this study were able to pass the course.

T ☐   F ☐   Line number: _____

4   To do extensive reading, you need to read a lot of challenging books.

T ☐   F ☐   Line number: _____

5   Reading enjoyable and rather easy books can improve overall reading skill and speed better than reading difficult texts.

T ☐   F ☐   Line number: _____

6   With extensive reading, you can improve your writing skills without even practising writing at all.

T ☐   F ☐   Line number: _____

7   Reading really helps your reading, writing, and vocabulary skills, but it does not help your speaking ability very much.

T ☐   F ☐   Line number: _____

8   Reading a lot in English can be more helpful in tests like TOEFL than actually living in an English-speaking country.

T ☐   F ☐   Line number: _____

COMPREHENSION 2   **Answer the questions without using a dictionary.**

1   In lines 4-5, what does the expression *far behind* mean?

   a   The students sat at the back of the class.
   b   The students took much longer to do the tests.
   c   The students had much lower test scores than other students.

2   Re-read the second paragraph. Which of the following is true?

   The students in the study …
   a   improved considerably in English and many enjoyed the class.
   b   didn't improve in English, but enjoyed the class.
   c   improved a little in English, but enjoyed the class.

3 Re-read the fourth paragraph. Which of the following is true?

   a Students who like reading and look for chances to read more are very likely to be successful language learners.

   b Students who read well have more opportunities to read and are more likely to enjoy it.

   c Students who do not enjoy reading or do not have the opportunity to read often can never become successful language learners.

4 In lines 35-36, which of the following expressions can replace the words *In short*?

   a For a short time

   b To summarize

   c In detail

   d To give a brief example

5 Re-read the sixth paragraph. Which of the following is implied?

   a Extensive reading cannot help advanced students with their writing skills.

   b Students with poor writing skills might not benefit from extensive reading.

   c To develop advanced writing skills, extensive reading might not be enough.

6 What is the best paraphrase of lines 50-52?

Extensive reading …

   a benefits reading and writing skills more than speaking and listening skills.

   b benefits speaking and listening for only a short time.

   c benefits speaking and listening skills more than reading and writing skills.

   d has very little benefit for speaking and listening skills.

7 According to lines 52-54, which of the following is true?

   a If a person reads a lot, in the future we know they will speak well.

   b If a person reads a lot, there is about a 50 per cent chance that they will also speak well.

   c We can make a fair guess as to whether a person speaks well, based on how much reading they do.

8 Re-read lines 61-66. Which of the following is true?

   a The longer you live in an English-speaking country, the better your TOEFL score is likely to be.

   b If you do not read very much, your TOEFL score is probably low.

   c People who have studied English for more than ten years usually perform better in TOEFL tests than those who have only studied for five years.

VOCABULARY FOCUS 1

Complete the sentences with the words in the box. Then ask and answer the questions with a partner.

reluctant

accuracy

effective

| accurately | term | oral | consistent |
| compulsory | reluctant | behind | effective |

1   How many English classes are you taking this _____?

2   Are you willing to approach and speak to a foreigner in English? Or are you rather _____ to do that?

3   Which do you think is more important, speaking English fluently or speaking English _____?

4   Do you think you would do better in a/an _____ evaluation of your English ability, or in a written evaluation?

5   Do you think your English ability is as good or better than most students your age, or are you falling _____?

6   It is important to study English in a good way. Do you know of any methods that are very _____?

7   Is the time you spend studying English each day _____, or does the amount of time you spend studying English change a lot from day to day?

8   Which classes are you taking this term that are _____? Which classes are you taking of your own choice?

VOCABULARY FOCUS 2

Complete the sentences with the appropriate form of the words in the box. One word is used more than once.

| take | make | receive | conduct | acquire |

1   Judith _____ impressive progress in her language ability just by watching a lot of films and TV programmes in English.

2   Some language teachers _____ experiments on their language classes.

3   Language students also _____ many benefits from extensive listening.

4   Maria _____ her English language skills while living in the United States.

5   Language experts need to _____ more research on the most effective ways to learn languages.

6   Students usually _____ the final test in the last class of term.

Grammar	This form is used to express the result of an extreme action or situation.
So … that …	… the students in the special class improved **so much that** their marks in the new tests were almost as high as the other English students'.

GRAMMAR 1   **Match the sentence halves to make logical statements.**

1   Jin-young studied so hard that she

2   Miguel stayed out so late that he

3   The bloke in front of me was so tall that I

4   Alyssa is so beautiful that every bloke

5   The film was so childish that I

a   wants to go out with her.

b   won a scholarship.

c   had to walk out after 30 minutes.

d   couldn't see the cinema screen.

e   couldn't wake up next morning.

GRAMMAR 2   **Complete the sentences with information about you.**

1   The best book I ever read was so _____ that I
_____.

2   I have a friend who is so _____ that everyone
_____.

3   My favourite film is so _____ that I _____.

4   The best teacher I've ever had was so _____ that
_____.

SPEAKING   **With a partner, think of some interesting and fun ways to improve these skills:**

• listening   • speaking   • writing

For example:

Listening to songs in English.

Effective • *Skills*

SCANNING **Scan the text to find the questions which give information about these topics.**

1 You question whether reading will really help your listening and speaking.   Question: _____

2 You wonder where you can find books for extensive reading.   Question: _____

3 You are worried mostly about IELTS-type tests.   Question: _____

4 You wonder if reading easy books is really better than reading challenging books.   Question: _____

5 You wonder how much you need to read to get any benefit.   Question: _____

EXTENSIVE READING Q&A

with Julian Bamford

Julian Bamford is a professor in the School of Information and Communications at Bunkyo University in Japan. He is the author of numerous books, articles, and studies about language learning, including several books about extensive reading. This week we asked him some of your questions.

Q1: *I know that for extensive reading I should read quite easy books. But wouldn't it be better if I read more challenging books with a lot of new vocabulary?*

A: Challenging books are useful. But are they enough? Do you
5   play a sport? If you want to be good at a sport, you need to practise, practise, practise. It's the same for reading. Extensive reading is practice. Challenging material is not good for practice. Imagine trying to practise tennis with a Wimbledon champion – you'd never be able to hit the ball! To practise, you need easy, interesting reading material,
10   and lots of it.

Q2: *I think that my weakest areas in English are speaking and listening. Will extensive reading really help me to develop these skills?*

A: We talk about grammar and vocabulary, about speaking and listening, and about reading and writing. But they are not separate.

15 English is all of them. Extensive reading strengthens your general English skills, so, yes, you become a better speaker and listener by reading. Is it better to just practise speaking and listening? It depends on you. The easiest way to learn English is to do what you like. Do you like reading? If so, do it. If not, do something else.

20 **Q3:** *Getting a good mark in IELTS is the most important thing to me at the moment. Can extensive reading really help? Isn't it better to go on some IELTS preparation courses?*

A: Extensive reading can help you with IELTS because it enables you to read faster and more confidently, and because it strengthens

25 your general English. An IELTS preparation course can also help you. Which is better for you? Well, perhaps you can do both, and a lot of other English activities as well!

Q4: *I have problems finding books that I can read without having to use a dictionary. Where can I find reading material that matches*

30 *my level?*

A: There are 'graded readers', which are intended for students to read without a dictionary. Choose a series of graded readers at the right level for you (most have about six levels, from very easy to difficult). If there are just a few unknown words on each page, that's

35 a good level for you. The best level is when you don't notice that you are reading in English. Try a higher level when you feel like it. If you are comfortable, stay at the new level. If not, stay at the old one.

Q5: *What is the minimum amount of reading that I have to do to benefit from extensive reading? Would twenty minutes a day be enough?*

40 *How about ten?*

A: How about five? There's no minimum or maximum. Like practising a sport, the more you practise, the more you benefit. The less practice, the less benefit. Why don't you read as much as you feel like today, and tomorrow, too? Extensive reading (unlike

45 most classroom reading) means reading fluently for general understanding. It does not mean a particular amount of reading – rather, it's a way of reading. A book a week (if the book is at a suitable level), is a common guideline. That should be enough to give you reading fluency, confidence, enjoyment, and some improvement

50 in language. If you want to be more ambitious about using extensive reading for language acquisition, some experts suggest about 100 pages a week (about twenty minutes reading per day, five days a week).

COMPREHENSION **Which of the opinions would Julian Bamford be most likely to agree with?**

1 Reading less than twenty minutes every day is not really helpful.

2 With extensive reading, you don't need to take IELTS preparation courses.

3 A good way to become a good reader is to read a lot.

4 Whenever possible, read books that are interesting for you.

5 Research has shown that extensive reading is the best way to learn a language.

6 When learning a language, it's very important to find methods that work best for you.

DISCUSSION **Reading gives you exposure to natural English, but listening to English as much as possible is also very useful. Look at the table and tick (✔) the appropriate boxes. Discuss your answers with a partner.**

English listening activity/advice	I already do this	I'd like to do this
Watch English-language programmes on TV		
Watch English-language films/DVDs		
Listen to English podcasts from the Internet		
Use CDs from English-language study materials		
Listen to English-language songs		
Download and listen to English files on my MP3 player		
Try to listen to English every day		
Do dictation exercises		
Other?		

4 • Money

PRE-READING 1 **What is most important to you in life? Put the following in order of importance, from 1 to 6.**

- ☐ having interests and hobbies
- ☐ spending time with your family
- ☐ having fun with your friends
- ☐ finding and being with your true love
- ☐ making money
- ☐ following a religion

PRE-READING 2 **Which of these opinions do you agree with? Discuss your answers with a partner.**

1 Rich people are usually happier than poor people. _____

2 In the United Kingdom, people were generally happier in the past than they are now. _____

3 People in Britain today have more money to spend than previous generations. _____

4 A salary increase has little effect on lasting happiness. _____

5 A pay cut can have a lasting impact on your happiness. _____

6 Making less money than your friends can affect your overall happiness. _____

Now read the text to find out what it says about the opinions above. Note the line numbers to show where you found the information.

The good life?

How much money do you need to be happy? For many, the answer to this question is simple: 'More!' Despite paying lip service to the notion that money and material things are secondary to family, love, and friends, people all around the world still pursue money as if it is the only thing that can make them happy. Everyone seems to be working harder and harder for more money at the expense of spending time with their families. People are spending more than ever before, and falling deeper and deeper into debt each year. We want bigger homes in better neighbourhoods, the latest cars, and bigger wide-screen TVs. It's 'the good life,' and everyone is clamouring to get it. But does having and spending a lot of money really make us happier?

Researchers have been interested for a long time in the link between income and happiness. Some conclude that once you have enough money to meet basic needs, such as food and shelter, having more money does little to help your happiness and general satisfaction with life. As a matter of fact, a recent study of 1,000 people in the United States found that those earning $1,000 or less a month were slightly happier than those whose monthly income was above $4,000.

In the West and in Asia, people own more and spend more than their parents' generation, yet some researchers claim that overall levels of happiness have remained even. While North Americans have twice as much spending power as they did in the 1950s, today they are ten times more likely to be depressed. Japan and Korea have become some of the wealthiest countries in the world, but they also have the third and fourth highest rates of suicide respectively, while countries with some of the highest rates of poverty often have the lowest rates of suicide. People are beginning to question the belief that wealth really makes our lives better. Indeed, the blind pursuit of being rich and consuming more and more products may actually do the reverse.

Why do more money and more things fail to make us happier? The problem is that we quickly get used to having more money and new things. Initially, we may feel euphoric when we get that bigger house or a new car, but we soon get used to having it, and then it doesn't seem so special any more. And when we hear that our friends or relatives now have bigger houses and newer cars, we become dissatisfied with what we have.

Indeed, money may be more effective in making us unhappy, rather than the other way around. An increase in salary may only produce temporary happiness, but getting a decrease in salary can adversely affect happiness in the long term. We become used to a certain level of

living and, when that is taken away, it is difficult for us to be satisfied with less.

Sociological researcher Glenn Firebaugh claims that it is not just a question of having or not having a lot of money. The key factor
45 is whether or not you have a lot of money compared to those around you. People can be quite satisfied with their salaries, for example, until they find out that their peers earn more. The desire to maintain equal or higher levels of income and purchasing habits as those around us (or 'keeping up with the Joneses', as the
50 common expression goes) turns life into a never-ending competition. Says Firebaugh, 'Rather than promoting overall happiness, continued income growth could promote an ongoing consumption race in which individuals consume more and more, just to maintain a constant level of happiness.'

55 Sociologists also point out that to earn a large amount of money we often have to sacrifice the things that really make us happy. Strong relationships, such as a loving family, a strong marriage and good friends are among the most powerful predictors of happiness and satisfaction with life. Simply finding what you love to do and
60 having time to do it is also a key factor. In most cases, the amount of money you earn has little effect on these things and quite often requires us to actually spend *less time* doing what really makes us happy. High-paying jobs tend to be very demanding, and can leave people with little energy for loved ones and hobbies.

65 So what place should money have in your life? This is entirely up to you, but consider what you would like to say when you look back on your life in your retirement. 'My marriage broke down, my children are strangers to me, and I usually felt miserable and stressed due to my high-powered job, but I drove the best car in
70 the neighbourhood!' Is that really what life is all about?

COMPREHENSION 1   **Each sentence in the summary has one mistake. Underline the mistakes. The first one has been done for you as an example.**

(**1**) Though <u>most</u> people claim money is more important to them than family and friends, many pursue money as if it is the most important thing in life. (**2**) However, in Asia and the United States, even though people today have more money, the levels of happiness are lower than before and levels of depression have greatly increased. (**3**) Generally, earning more money and buying new things helps one become happier only in the long term. (**4**) One researcher found that earning less money than others you compare yourself with has a positive effect on your happiness. (**5**) Finally, researchers claim that well-paid jobs usually give you more time to be with your loved ones. (**6**) In conclusion, the author infers that at the end of your life, good relationships with your family are less important than the things you owned.

COMPREHENSION 2   **Answer the questions.**

1   In line 2, what does the expression *paying lip service to* mean?

a   People often say that money is more important than family, friends, and love.

b   People say money is not that important, but pay for a lot of services that they think will make them happy.

c   People might say family, friends, and love are the most important things in their lives, but they behave as though money is the most important thing.

2   Which is the best paraphrase of lines 5–7?

a   People work harder because it is expensive to do things with their families.

b   People work harder for more money, but this results in less time to spend with their families.

c   People want to spend more time with their families, so they work harder.

3   In lines 20–21, *overall levels of happiness have remained even* means …

a   the percentage of happy people has neither increased nor decreased.

b   the number of happy people is still fair and appropriate.

c   the number of people who are happy is not an odd number.

4   What is the best paraphrase of lines 23–26?

a   Japan has the third highest suicide rate in the world and Korea has the fourth.

b   Korea has the third highest suicide rate in the world and Japan has the fourth.

5 In line 28, what does *blind pursuit* mean?

    a Trying to get something without really understanding why you want it.

    b Trying to get something, but you do not know how to do it.

    c Trying to get something that you can't see.

6 What is the best paraphrase of lines 37–38?

    a Money can make us unhappy in ways we do not expect.

    b Money might have more power to make us unhappy than to make us happy.

    c Money might make us feel unhappy and lost.

7 What is the *ongoing consumption race* that is described in lines 52-53?

    a People continually compete with others to buy more and more products, just so they can remain satisfied.

    b A situation in which people buy more and more things, and thus increase their level of happiness continually.

    c A situation in which businesses encourage people to buy more products, thereby keeping the economy strong and people happy.

8 What does the phrase *up to you* (lines 65–66) mean?

    a It is out of your control.

    b It is unknown to you.

    c It is your choice.

SPEAKING   **Which of the following best represents your opinion of the text?**

1 I strongly disagree. I still think we need a lot of money to be happy.

2 I generally disagree. Money is not everything, but it is still important for my happiness.

3 I generally agree. It is good to have money, but true happiness comes from other things.

4 I completely agree. Too many people have difficult lives because they value money too much.

VOCABULARY FOCUS 1   **Complete the sentences with the expressions in the box. Discuss your answers with a partner.**

bother me a lot   bother me a bit   not bother me at all

1 It would _____ if I wasn't quite rich in future.

2 It would _____ if my friends earned more money than I did in the future.

3 It would _____ if my child married someone who was poor.

VOCABULARY
FOCUS 2

wealth

satisfied

temporary

Complete the sentences with the words in the box. Then ask and answer the questions with a partner.

sacrifice	wealth	debt	temporary
logically	satisfied	earn	income

1 Have you ever borrowed money and fallen into _____?

2 Do you believe that money can bring lasting happiness or is it just _____?

3 Having money is great, but would you choose _____ before love?

4 What would you never _____ just for more money: family, friends, free time, or true love?

5 When it comes to love, do you act emotionally or _____?

6 Have you ever had a part-time job? How much money did you _____?

7 Would you be _____ with your life if you never had a lot of money? Or would you always feel disappointed?

8 What kind of job gives a high _____, but also allows you a lot of free time?

VOCABULARY
FOCUS 3

Complete the sentences with correct words.

1 *satisfaction* (n)/*satisfied* (adj)

   a I would be _____ with a B for this work.

   b I would have more _____ if I got an A.

2 *pursuit* (n)/*pursue* (v)

   a Money isn't everything. Some people also _____ fame.

   b Achieving success in life is a common _____.

3 *initial* (adj)/*initially* (adv)

   a _____ I thought she was intelligent, but now I know she isn't.

   b Sometimes our _____ impressions are wrong!

4 *depressed* (adj)/*depression* (n)

   a When couples break up, they often experience _____.

   b It's hard not to be _____ when someone you love leaves you.

5 *stressed* (adj)/*stress* (n)

   a I really am _____ at the moment because I have so much homework.

   b All this _____ is exhausting!

6 *failure* (n)/*fail* (v)

   a It is not a bad thing to _____.

   b We can learn a lot from _____.

Grammar	*Despite* and *even though* have the same meaning, but are used in grammatically different ways in sentences.
Despite and *even though*	*Despite* is a preposition, and is followed by a noun phrase. They kept playing **despite the rain.** **Despite the fact** that they love each other, they decided not to get married. **Despite losing** the game, the players still had a good time. *Even though* introduces a clause. His plans failed, **even though he had done his best.** **Even though we know smoking is harmful**, a lot of us still smoke.

GRAMMAR 1   **Combine the sentences using *even though*. Be careful to use *even though* in the correct clause, so the sentence is logical.**

For example:

He won a lot of money. He is still dissatisfied.

Even though he won a lot of money, he is still dissatisfied.

or

He is still dissatisfied, even though he won a lot of money.

1   The musician Ray Charles was blind. He became a very famous songwriter and musician.

2   Bill Gates became the richest man in the world. He left Harvard University before graduating.

3   Japan, Korea, and Taiwan were very poor after the Second World War. They are some of the wealthiest countries in the world today.

4   Amy was unable to gain a place at university. She didn't stop trying.

GRAMMAR 2   **Combine the sentences using *despite*.**

1   The weather is bad. We will still go hiking.

2   It is a fact that Luke is not good looking. He has a beautiful girlfriend.

3   He had a leg injury. He kept playing in the football match.

4   The temperature is very low at the moment. Some people still aren't wearing coats.

SPEAKING   **Complete the sentences with information about you. Discuss your answers with a partner.**

1   Even though my English isn't perfect yet, I can still _____.

2   Despite the problems and challenges I might face, one day I will _____.

3   I can find ways to be satisfied with my life, even though _____.

4   I hope I can get my dream job in the future, despite the fact that _____.

Effective • *Skills*

SCANNING **Scan the text. Read the first sentence only in paragraphs 2–5. Write the key expressions for the topics in each paragraph.**

For example:

Paragraph 2: _____*approval of others*_____

Paragraph 3: _____

Paragraph 4: _____

Paragraph 5: _____

Paragraph 6: _____

What specific arguments will you find in the text?

MONEY MATTERS

Money can't buy happiness. Money can't buy us love. Rich people supposedly aren't that much happier than the poor. Wealth can never replace relationships, family ties, the good feeling we get from helping others, etc. We've all heard this before time and time again, but let's be realistic. Though money may not be everything, in the United States it really does have an effect on happiness.

First of all, money brings respect and approval from others. People might say that we should not be so concerned about what others think of us, and that happiness can only come from within. Yet that's far easier said than done. Realistically, very few people can live happily without the approval of others. For most, it does and it will always bother us when we are looked down on, perhaps because we drive an old car or live in a small, cheap flat. True, the initial thrill of buying a new car might fade away, but the car itself is a status symbol that others respect, and this effect is not as temporary. It isn't easy to accept being middle class or poor when richer people seem to command immediate respect and esteem, just because they are financially successful. We can't help but want it as well.

We should also bear in mind that money is a symbol of ability and achievement. If you are a talented athlete, musician, writer, business person, and so on, it is likely that your ability will bring financial rewards. But while you gain satisfaction from having your talent recognized and rewarded, it may not be the money itself which makes you happy.

Furthermore, money allows us to live in an environment which can promote happiness. How happy could you be, living in the dangerous and dirty environment in which poor people usually have to live? If you have money, you can live in a safe, clean, and beautiful place. You'll have good schools and parks nearby for your children, and easy access to vital facilities like hospitals. How can these things not contribute to your happiness?

Perhaps money cannot buy love, but a lack of money can certainly make it harder to find love. The more money you earn, the better chance you have of finding a good marriage partner. Let's face it; if you are rich, you will have a bigger choice of partners. If you are poor, you will have fewer opportunities to find a mate. Nowadays more women are financially independent, so you would expect this not to be the case. However, it is a fact that if you are a man and do not have money, or at least show that you are likely to earn a reasonable amount of money in future, many women will not give you a chance.

Finally, and perhaps most importantly, money allows you to provide for your children. People with money always make sure that their children live in healthy environments and get the best education possible. Poor families simply cannot compete, and their children are much more likely to fail academically. This results in fewer prospects for the future. This is the information age, and education is more important than ever for survival. How would you feel if you had a bright son or daughter who could be anything he or she wanted, but who will never get the chance simply because you cannot afford to give him or her a good education? How can you be happy knowing that your children will be unable to fulfil their potential?

Oscar Wilde, the famous Irish novelist, once said, 'When I was young, I used to think money was important in life. Now, being old, I know it is.' In reality, few people have the courage and ability to resist the influence of money, and to live truly happy and fulfilled lives. In the United States, people without money live lives filled with stress, anxiety, and frustration. That's just the way it is. So, you can keep all your talk about money not making people happy. From where I stand, the clear conclusion to this debate is that money does indeed matter. It always has, and it always will.

SUMMARY AND REFLECTION

Answer the questions in your own words. How much do you agree with each point?

1 What is the main point of the essay?

2 What is the first argument (para. 2)?

3 What is the second argument (para. 3)?

4 What is the third argument (para. 4)?

5 What is the fourth argument (para. 5)?

6 What is the fifth argument (para. 6)?

DICTIONARY
SKILLS Use the information from the dictionary entries for each of the words below to choose the grammatically correct sentence. (Look at the model sentences in the dictionary entries for clues.)

1 *lack*

    a I am lack of free time these days.

    b I lack free time these days.

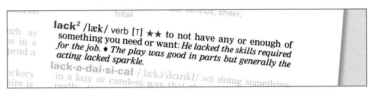

2 *potential*

    a She has great potential to be rich one day.

    b She has great potentials to be rich one day.

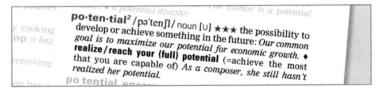

3 *influence*

    a He influenced to me for being a good person.

    b He influenced me to be a good person.

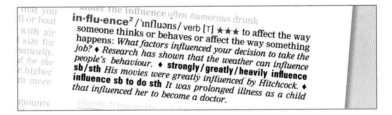

4 *resist*

    a Most people can't resist wanting more money.

    b Most people can't resist to want more money.

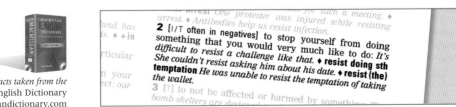

Extracts taken from the
Macmillan English Dictionary
www.macmillandictionary.com

EXERCISE 1

Read the text.

Read and succeed!

The French **philosopher**, René Descartes, wrote, 'The reading of all good books is like a conversation with all the finest men of past centuries.' American humourist Will Rogers observed, 'A man only learns in two ways, one by reading, and the other by association with smarter people.' People have always appreciated the educational value of reading, but recent research also suggests that reading habits can have an effect on our spending as well. One study found that children and adolescents who had good reading habits were more likely to be successful as adults. Another study found that people from low-income families who liked to read as children and **adolescents** were more likely to increase their financial and social position when they became adults than those who did not. According to a United States government survey on reading in 2002, levels of income **correlated** very strongly with reading habits: people who read a lot tended to have higher incomes than those who did not read often. The American Success Institute lists reading as a key component in 'mastering life,' their tenth **principle** of success.

EXERCISE 2

Answer the questions.

1 What is the main point of the text?

   a Reading is a very effective way of developing communication skills.

   b Reading can have a strong effect on income.

   c Good reading habits can make people rich.

   d Reading is the best way to become knowledgeable and educated.

2 Which of the following are mentioned in the text? <u>Underline</u> all the correct answers.

   a Reading a lot can have a positive effect on your career.

   b People who read often are more likely to be rich than people who do not read often.

   c People who enjoy reading are usually better at saving and spending money than those who do not read often.

   d Children from poor families who enjoy reading are likely to have better jobs than their parents.

   e People who read English well have access to more information than those who cannot read in English.

3 Which of the following can be inferred from the text?

   a Schools are not teaching children appropriate reading skills.

   b People are reading more now than ever before.

   c Good reading habits need to be developed before a person becomes a teenager.

   d Developing good reading habits is one of the most important things families and schools can do for children.

EXERCISE 3

Match the key words in bold in the text to the correct definitions (1–4).

1 When two things are connected to each other in some way.

   _____

2 Teenagers who are changing from children to adults.

   _____

3 Someone who studies and writes about the meaning of life.

   _____

4 A basic belief, theory, or rule that influences the way something is done.

   _____

EXERCISE 1

Read the text and answer the questions in Exercise 2 as quickly as you can. Write your starting and finishing time.

Start time: _____

Finish time: _____

The frugal student

For most university students, financial resources are limited. To make the most of your money, it is a good idea to keep track of your spending habits. Keeping a record of where your money goes is a good way to reduce unnecessary expenses. Many people are surprised to find that it is usually small things, such as snacks and cups of coffee at Starbucks, that take a big bite out of their budget. Once you know where your money is going, making a realistic spending plan and sticking to it is the next step. List all your sources of income and compare them with your expenses. You will probably have to make some painful decisions, but it will help you to establish good spending habits that will make your life easier long after your university days are over.

EXERCISE 2

Decide if the sentences are True (T), False (F), or if the information is Not Given (NG) in the text.

1   This text is mainly about saving money for college.

    T ☐   F ☐   NG ☐

2   The author suggests that university students should stop drinking coffee to save money.

    T ☐   F ☐   NG ☐

3   Students do not need to worry about things that don't cost much.

    T ☐   F ☐   NG ☐

4   The text suggests finding out how you usually spend your money before you set a budget.

    T ☐   F ☐   NG ☐

5   Those who save money at university are usually financially successful later in life.

    T ☐   F ☐   NG ☐

6   The author implies that the advice is always useful, even after students have graduated.

    T ☐   F ☐   NG ☐

EXERCISE 3

Complete the text with the words in the box. Use each word once only.

sacrifice   debt   income   afford
cost   bank loans   earn   wealth

A major problem in Britain is the ever growing (1)_____ of education. Families that do not have a high (2)_____ often have to (3)_____ many things, such as free time and holidays to pay for their children's lessons and teachers. It is not uncommon for entire families to move, just so that their children can go to better schools. To (4)_____ more money, both parents usually have one or even two jobs. Other families spend more than they can (5)_____, so it is easy to fall into (6)_____ with (7)_____ and credit card bills. Considering the costs of education, is it a surprise that (8)_____ is so highly valued these days?

5 · Love

PRE-READING 1 **Complete the sentences with the key words in bold from the text.**

1   Marriage should be considered a strong _____, and a promise that a couple will work hard to love and take care of each other.

2   Jennifer is _____ to Darren. Unfortunately, Darren isn't interested in Jennifer.

3   Ann doesn't like flowers as presents. She prefers _____ gifts that are useful.

4   When a _____ ends, one person usually has a broken heart.

5   He has a real _____ for music. He can't live without it!

6   People with broken hearts develop a bad _____ to love for a while.

PRE-READING 2 **Here are four quotes about love. Which do you agree with? Discuss your answers with a partner.**

1   *All's fair in love and war.* Francis Edward Smedley

2   *Everybody in love is blind.* Propertius

3   *Love is the flower of life, and blossoms unexpectedly and without law, and must be plucked where it is found, and enjoyed for the brief hour of its duration.* D.H. Lawrence

4   *All love that has not friendship for its base, is like a mansion built upon sand.* Ella Wheeler Wilcox

PRE-READING 3 **Read the text and find out which love style is yours.**

The six styles of love

'Everyone admits that love is wonderful and necessary, yet no one agrees on just what it is.' Diane Ackerman (author)

'All you need is love,' the Beatles sang back in the 1960s. A bit overstated, perhaps, but people generally agree that love is one of the most important things in life. However, just exactly what love is may depend on whom you ask, as psychologists have found that love means different things to different people.

Psychologist John Alan Lee identified six love style categories in the early 1970s, each representing a different purpose and **attitude** about love that most people have. Building on Lee's work, psychology professors Susan and Clyde Hendrick created the *Love Attitudes Scale*: a survey which helps people identify their love style. They claim that understanding which style of love you most closely match can increase the odds of you finding your own Mr or Mrs Right.

The passionate Eros
The Eros-type lover is the passionate lover often written about in romance novels. People with a high degree of the Eros style have an intense focus on their partner that can last for years and years. Eros lovers have a very definite image of what they want for a partner and, once they find this person, they go all out to win his or her love. If you find yourself only **attracted** to a specific kind of person, then you might have some aspects of Eros in you.

The player Ludus
Ludus are the type of lovers your mother warned you about. They look at love as a game and often cannot limit themselves to just one partner at a time. The Ludus does not have any specific preferences and flirts with almost everyone. Ludus lovers have a problem with commitment and often end **relationships** when things are going 'too well'. Though Ludus-style lovers are often looked down on, the Hendricks point out that most just want to have a good time and rarely intend to hurt anyone.

The stable and safe Storge (pronounced *stor-gae*)
To the Storge-type lover, friendship, **commitment**, and security are more important than heated romance and physical attraction. For Storges, love is a safe, comfortable relationship with a person who shares similar goals and outlooks on life. Their relationships usually begin as friends and slowly develop into deeper feelings of love. Physical intimacy and wild **passion** are often lacking in Storge relationships, yet their relationships are the most likely to endure.

The practical Pragma

Pragma-style lovers are very **practical** when it comes to love and relationships. Pragmas have a clear image of what kind of life they want and look for a partner who will help them attain it. Pragmas have a 'shopping list' approach to relationships and 'shop' for mates with specific qualities such as type of occupation, family background, and personality. It may seem cold and calculating, but Pragmas consider this approach simply realistic. They are similar to Storges in that they put less emphasis on passion and romance, but Pragma lovers have pre-conditions for relationships, while Storges often find love comes naturally from friendships.

The self-destructive Manic

As the name suggests, this type of lover is a bit unstable emotionally. 'A Manic lover yearns for love, but somehow it always becomes painful,' says Susan. 'This lover is jealous and full of doubts about his or her partner's commitment. They also experience dramatic physical symptoms, like the inability to eat and sleep.' Manic lovers often push away partners by their possessive behaviour, and are unable to relax and allow the relationship to evolve naturally. Thus, often the Manic's own actions make their worst fear, that their lover will leave them, become reality.

The saintly Agape

The rarest of love styles is the Agapic lover. 'The Agapic lover is the closest thing the romantic world has to a saint,' says Susan. Agapic lovers are able to put the needs of their lover before their own. They ask for little from their partner, seeking only to give as much as they can. Agape lovers can sometimes sacrifice too much, however, and may feel unappreciated by their partners.

Couples with similar love styles do tend to form longer-lasting relationships, as they often share the same ideals and goals. 'Essentially, the more similar two people are on most relevant variables, the more likely the relationship is to be satisfying and stable. One exception might be Mania, where a Manic partner might be better balanced by a partner higher in Storge or Agape,' Susan explains. 'A Manic lover might be fine as long as the partner is willing to give extra attention and reassurance to help him or her feel more secure.'

However, couples with different love styles can still form successful unions. 'Knowing that your partner has a different love style or sexual style than you do can enhance communication and understanding,' Susan explains. The Hendricks also note that most people are a mix of love styles, and that love styles are not 'fixed in the genes'. 'We proposed that love styles are attitudes, not personality. Thus there is always the potential for change.'

COMPREHENSION 1 Identify the most likely love style of each of the people below.

1 When Cynthia falls in love, she can't help but think about her boyfriend all the time. She often worries about how much he loves her.

_____

2 Even after three years of being together, John likes to treat his girlfriend to romantic dinners and surprise her with gifts.

_____

3 David is a very busy man. He is dating two girls right now and he is even considering asking out a third girl on a date.

_____

4 Eric's girlfriend does not treat him very well. He understands her, though, and knows that she needs his patience and love.

_____

5 Samantha just broke up with her new boyfriend. She found out that he wants to have more than one child someday, and that is not what she has in mind for her future family.

_____

6 Monica doesn't know exactly when she and her boyfriend fell in love. They just spent a lot of time with each other and, after a few years, realized they loved each other.

_____

COMPREHENSION 2 Answer the questions.

1 Which of the following best summarizes lines 5–7?

a There is no one answer to what love is. You get a different answer from each person.

b You have to ask the right person to find out what love is.

c Only psychologists and experts really know what love is.

2 In line 10, which expression means _to add to or continue the work of someone before?_

_____

3 In the paragraph 'The player Ludus', which word means _to act towards someone in a way that shows you are attracted to them_?

_____

4 What is the best paraphrase of _Though Ludus-style lovers are often looked down on_ … (line 29)?

a Most people see Ludus lovers as dangerous.

b Most people judge Ludus lovers as being bad.

c Ludus lovers often try to find many girlfriends/boyfriends.

d Ludus lovers are not easy to find.

5 Re-read lines 47–50. Which of the following is true?

   a Pragma lovers want people to be a certain way before they even consider being with them.

   b Pragma lovers spend a lot of time preparing themselves for new relationships.

   c Pragma lovers try to find out a lot of information about new people before they will date them.

6 In which lines is there an example of how a Manic lover might be *self-destructive*?

_____

7 Re-read lines 71–75. Which of the following is true?

   a Manic lovers are especially good together.

   b The opposite of a Manic lover is a Storge or Agape lover.

   c Storge and Agape lovers can help a Manic lover overcome his/her weaknesses.

8 Re-read the last paragraph. Which of the following is true?

   a Our love styles cannot be changed by medical treatments.

   b Our loves styles can be changed by our efforts.

   c Our love styles are constantly changing.

SPEAKING   **Discuss the questions with a partner.**

1 Which love style or styles do you closely match?

2 Which love styles would be OK for your future partner? Which love styles would you avoid when looking for a partner?

3 If you found out your new boyfriend/girlfriend was a Ludos or Manic lover in previous relationships, would you still give him/her a chance?

VOCABULARY FOCUS 1   **Match words (1–5) to their antonyms (a–e).**

unemotional

passionate

1 destroy		**a**	disappointing
2 relevant		**b**	create
3 intense		**c**	unemotional
4 passionate		**d**	weak
5 satisfying		**e**	unimportant

unappreciated

Match the words (6–10) to their synonyms (f–j).

6	emphasis	**f**	not respected
7	evolve	**g**	importance
8	wild	**h**	angelic
9	unappreciated	**i**	out of control
10	saintly	**j**	develop

VOCABULARY FOCUS 2 Use the dictionary entries to identify the correct meaning of these words as they are used in the text on pages 51–52.

1 attract (line 21)   Entry: _____

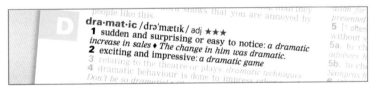

sth What first attracted you to the study of Buddhism? ♦ **attract sb to**
1a. to produce or cause an interest in something or someone, or have an opinion about them: *Their behaviour has attracted considerable public criticism.* ♦ *Their attempts to attract the support of peasants and workers failed.* ♦ **attract sb's attention** *They tried to leave the hotel without attracting anyone's attention.* **1b.** [usually passive] to interest someone in a romantic or sexual way: **be attracted to sb** *She's old enough now to be attracted to boys.* **2** to make something move near someone or something: *Insects are often* ...

2 endure (line 39)   Entry: _____

that irritated Lydia almost beyond endurance.
en·dure /ɪnˈdʊr/ verb ★ [T] to suffer something unpleasant or difficult in a patient way over a long period: *He endured solitude and torture for months at a time.* **a.** [I] to last for a long time: *traditions that endure* —**en·dur·a·ble** adj
en·dur·ing /ɪnˈdʊrɪŋ/ adj ...

3 dramatic (line 55)   Entry: _____

people like this.
dra·mat·ic /drəˈmætɪk/ adj ★★★
1 sudden and surprising or easy to notice: *a dramatic increase in sales* ♦ *The change in him was dramatic.*
2 exciting and impressive: *a dramatic game*
3 relating to the theatre or plays: *dramatic techniques*
4 dramatic behaviour is done to impress others: *Don't be so dramatic!* ...

4 fixed (line 80)   Entry: _____

from changing **2** a type of glue
fixed /fɪkst/ adj ★★
1 something such as an amount, date, or time that is fixed has been agreed on and will not change: *a fixed price* ♦ *The contract is for a fixed period of three years.* ♦ *The interest rate on the loan is fixed.* **1a.** a fixed expression on someone's face does not change or look natural: *a fixed smile* **1b.** a fixed idea or opinion does not change although it may be wrong: *My mother has fixed ideas about how to bring up children.*
2 something that is fixed is fastened ...

Extracts taken from the Macmillan English Dictionary www.macmillandictionary.com

Grammar	Clauses with *in that* give an explanation of the preceding clause. They are common when making comparisons.
In that clauses	*Pragma lovers are similar to Storge **in that** they put less emphasis on romance.*
	*Eros lovers are different from Ludus **in that** they are only attracted to specific types of people.*

GRAMMAR 1 **Match the sentence halves to make logical statements.**

1 The United States is similar to Canada in that

2 Canada is different from the United States in that

3 Field hockey is similar to ice hockey in that

4 Field hockey is different from ice hockey in that

a players use sticks to hit the ball or puck.

b it has two official languages: English and French.

c English is the most commonly spoken language.

d it uses a penalty-card system for players who break the rules.

GRAMMAR 2 **Complete the sentences with information about you.**

1 I am similar to my _____ in that _____.

2 I am different from my _____ in that _____.

3 My university life is different from my secondary school life in that _____.

4 My life now is different from five years ago in that _____.

GRAMMAR 3 **Write three more sentences using *in that*. Discuss your answers with a partner.**

_____

_____

_____

Effective • *Skills*

PERSONALIZATION You have a first date with someone that you are very interested in. What would you worry about the most? Brainstorm a list with your partner.

I would worry about . . . _____

Does the text mention the problems you discussed?

For the perfect first date

You finally did it. You have a date with that perfect someone whom you've **had your eye on** for weeks. Finally, you have the chance to start what could be a great romance that may even turn out to be the love of your life. But what if the date doesn't go well? What if you say
5 the wrong thing? What if he or she finds you boring? In short, what if you **blow it**?

For most people, first dates can be extremely stressful. So, what can you do to increase your odds of success? The following are some tips that can help you **land** the guy or gal of your dreams.

10 **1. Have the right attitude**
You'll find dating to be a much more pleasurable and rewarding experience if you just relax and try to have fun. If you feel a lot of pressure for the date to succeed, you'll probably be too tense and not make a good impression. Going to the other extreme, pretending not
15 to care at all, can be even worse. Think of dating as simply a fun opportunity to get to know people and yourself. If things work out, great. If they don't, you'll learn from the experience and do better next time. Smile, **stay upbeat**, and let yourself have fun.

2. Choose the right place
20 The usual 'dinner and cinema' is not always the best choice for a first date. You can't really get to know someone while your **eyes are glued to** a cinema screen. Also, if the file happens to be bad, it can create a negative mood for the whole date. Make the date special by going to a

museum, art gallery, or any outdoor event. The atmosphere is pleasant
and peaceful, and it is easy to make conversation by chatting about
the interesting things you see in these places. Amusement parks can
also be a good choice, as they make most people feel lively and
carefree; the perfect mood to create if you want to start a romance!

3. Let your partner do most of the talking

One major source of stress on dates is keeping the conversation lively and
interesting. The last thing you want on a date is an awkward silence.
However, don't talk about yourself all night long, either. You'll **come across
as** either arrogant or insecure (people who really do have ability and
confidence do not need to advertise it). Try to focus the conversation on
the other person and be an attentive listener. Not only does this make the
conversation interesting for your partner, but you'll also get to know the
person much better (that's why you are on the date **in the first place**,
remember!).

4. Talk about the right things

A lot of people make the mistake of asking questions only about
typical and predictable topics, such as school and family. These are the
standard questions like, 'How long have you lived here?' and 'So, how
do you like your classes this term?' These questions are not bad, but if
you only ask this kind of question, you'll find your date yawning and
looking at his or her watch often.

Questions that demand a little thinking and lead to interesting answers
are the key. 'What activities do you do that make you most relaxed?'
'If you had an extra hour of free time each day, how would you spend it?'
This kind of question helps people **open up** and overcome being shy or
nervous. Before the date, have a number of questions like these in mind
that you can ask when things start to get a bit slow. Be prepared to
answer those questions yourself as well!

Otherwise, try to find a topic that both of you find interesting and let
the conversation flow from there. If you can't find any topics that you
have in common, you probably do not have much of a chance for a
good relationship anyway.

Finally, don't ask or talk about previous relationships. People who talk
about their previous relationships usually haven't **got over them** yet.
If you complain about your ex, your date will think you still have some
emotional issues and are not ready for a new relationship.

COMPREHENSION **Which of these situations follow the advice in the text? Explain your answers.**

1 Ken takes his date to the zoo.

2 Yvette asks a lot of questions about her date's college and classes.

3 Kimberley asks her date which famous person he respects the most.

4 Brandon decides to impress his date by talking about all of his achievements in sports and school.

UNDERSTANDING VOCABULARY FROM CONTEXT **Match the expressions in bold in the text (1–10) to their meanings (a–j) without using a dictionary.**

1 have your eye on something

2 blow it

3 land

4 stay upbeat

5 eyes are glued to

6 come across as

7 in the first place

8 open up

9 have in common

10 get over someone

a Focus on something strongly

b Forget about past problems and be happy

c Remain positive

d Fail, lose a good opportunity

e Initially, the original situation

f Achieve something you desire

g Be perceived as, to give a certain impression

h Talk freely about your feelings, not be private

i Sharing the same interests

j Have something you plan or wish to obtain

6 • The Internet

Complete the sentences with the key words in bold from the text.

1 Noam Chomsky is one of the most famous _____ today. He has proposed many theories about language learning.

2 The computer got a virus and now all the files are _____. They are completely unusable and need to be made again.

3 I can't understand my teenage son when he writes emails to me. He uses too much _____.

4 When I was young, we played a lot of sports in our free time. The younger _____, however, seems to spend more time playing computer games and surfing the Internet.

5 In England, the dialect of the language spoken in London is considered _____. That is the English language you hear on TV and read in most newspapers.

6 Is television a threat to _____? Or do people still read and write as well as they have in the past?

Discuss the questions with a partner.

1 When young people in your country write on the Internet and send text messages, what kind of non-standard language do they use (new spelling, grammar, words, etc.)? Share some examples with your partner.

2 In many countries around the world, teachers and parents often complain about the way young people change the language when using electronic communication (Internet, text messages, etc.). Do you think this is a problem?
Why?/Why not?

Is Netspeak harming the English language?

My summr hols wr CWOT. B4, we usd 2 go 2 NY 2C my bro, his GF & thr 3 :-@ kids FTF. ILNY, its gr8.

Can you understand this sentence? If you can't, don't feel too bad: neither could the middle school teacher in Scotland who received this
5   as homework from one of her students. This is **Netspeak**: the language of computerized communication found in Internet chat rooms, instant messages (IM), and text messages on mobile phones. Netspeak is a collection of abbreviations (cuz = *because*), acronyms (BRB = *Be Right Back*), and symbols (C U B4 clss = *see you before*
10 *class*). To newcomers (*newbies* in Netspeak), it can look like a completely foreign language. So, what is the 'translation' of the sentence above? *My summer holidays were a complete waste of time. Before, we used to go to New York to see my brother, his girlfriend, and their three screaming kids face to face. I love New York; it's great.*

15 Language purists, schoolteachers, and parents everywhere say this new form of writing, with its disregard for proper spelling, punctuation, and grammar, threatens to destroy the English language. It is blamed for a perceived increase in spelling and grammatical errors in students' writing in school work. School boards, teachers, and
20 parent groups call for zero tolerance of Netspeak, for fear that the writing of the new generation might become completely incomprehensible and the language itself could become **corrupted**.

Everyone should just relax, say **linguists** and language scholars. While there certainly is a need to ensure students learn the **standard**
25 rules of writing, the phenomenon of Netspeak and writing on the Internet, they claim, is actually doing more good than harm.

David Crystal, a language historian at the University of Wales in the UK, argues that Netspeak and the Internet are developing new forms of creative language use that provide a strong motivation for **literacy** (the
30 skills of reading and writing). Crystal points out that through personal home pages and weblogs (commonly known as *blogs*), the almost lost art of diary keeping has been revived. Stanford University linguist Geoffrey Nunberg agrees. 'People get better at writing by writing,' he claims, and online chatting and instant messages are getting young
35 people to write more than ever before. 'I think you could argue that the kids who are now doing text messaging, email, and instant messages will end up writing at least as well as, and possibly better than, their parents or than any **generation** in history.'

40 Linguists further argue that electronic messages should be considered a new medium of communication and not judged on the standard rules of writing. This new medium has features of both spoken and written English, but has more in common with speaking than traditional writing due to its nearly instantaneous, interactive nature.
45 Like spoken language, it is considerably shorter, utilizes a more limited range of vocabulary, and is more relaxed in grammar rules.

Linguist James Milroy notes that people have been complaining about the supposed decline in English for centuries. Every generation, without exception, has believed that young people are destroying the language. And you can bet your bottom dollar that
50 when today's teenagers become tomorrow's parents, they too will accuse their children of ruining the language. Milroy argues that there is no evidence that young people have any deficiency in their language in comparison with previous generations. From a linguist's point of view, languages do not and cannot become 'corrupted'; they
55 simply change to meet the needs of each new generation.

However, Netspeak enthusiasts do acknowledge the importance of teaching young people how to speak and write proper English. 'Children have to be taught about their language,' Crystal said. 'They have to learn about the importance of Standard English as a medium
60 of educated communication.' Cynthia McVey, psychology lecturer at Glasgow Caledonian University, agrees. 'I can understand the frustration of teachers and I think it's important that they get across to their pupils that text messaging is for fun, but that learning to write proper English is vital for their career or future study.'

65 Perhaps we should give teenagers a little more credit anyway. Erin, aged 12, has become fluent in Netspeak in just two months, but knows it is not appropriate to use it in school. 'I wouldn't use text language in my homework. Texting is for fun, not for school, and I think you would have to be a bit silly to get them mixed up.'

COMPREHENSION 1 **Complete the summary with the words in the box. Use each word only once.**

harming	creativity	standard	concerned
change	Netspeak	encourages	corrupted

Many educators and parents are (**1**)_____ that the younger generation is corrupting English through (**2**)_____; the language young people use to communicate on the Internet and through text messages on their mobile phones. Language experts, however, claim that Netspeak is not (**3**)_____, but actually helping the language. For one thing, it develops (**4**)_____ with the language, and secondly it (**5**)_____ more writing. Experts claim that all generations believe their language is being (**6**)_____ by new generations. In reality, languages do not become 'bad,' but only (**7**)_____. Linguists do say, however, that (**8**) _____ writing skills should be taught in schools, and that students should know when and when not to use Netspeak.

COMPREHENSION 2 | **Answer the questions without using a dictionary.**

1   In line 15, *purists* means …

    a people who are honest and good.

    b people who want to keep something unchanged.

    c people who are expert at something.

2   Reread lines 16–17. Which of the following is true?

    a Netspeak has a different, but creative system of spelling and grammar.

    b Netspeak does not use traditional spelling and grammar.

    c The spelling and grammar of Netspeak makes communication difficult.

3   What is the best paraphrase of lines 19–20?

    a They want the use of Netspeak to be reduced in the classroom.

    b They want absolutely no Netspeak used in the classroom.

    c They want people to use Netspeak wisely in the classroom.

4   What is the definition of the word *literacy* in paragraph 4?

    _____

5   In lines 36–38, which expression means *in the end, eventually*?

    _____

6   Why is the word *supposed* used in line 47?

    a The author wants to stress that the reader should agree that the English language is in decline.

    b The author expects that the English language will decline.

    c The author questions the idea that there is a decline in the English language.

7   In line 49, what does *bet your bottom dollar* mean?

    a You can be certain of something.

    b You can make a lot of money at something.

    c There is a good chance that something will happen.

8   In line 65, what is the author suggesting about teenagers?

    a They just need more time.

    b We should give them more support.

    c We should trust them a little more.

SPEAKING | **Discuss the questions with a partner.**

1 Choose the response that most closely matches your own opinion.

   a I agree strongly with the text.

   b I tend to agree with the text, but there are one or two things I am not sure about.

   c I tend to disagree with the text. It has a few good points, but generally I think Netspeak causes too many problems.

   d I disagree with the text completely. I don't think there are any real benefits of Netspeak.

2 Do you use your native language version of Netspeak often? Can you understand it well?

VOCABULARY FOCUS 1 | **Complete the questions with the words in the box. Then ask and answer the questions with a partner.**

blame	generations	complain
harms	considerably	motivation

1 Do you think Netspeak _____ language? Or do you think it is helping it?

2 Do you sometimes find it difficult to communicate with older _____, like your grandparents?

3 Do you _____ Netspeak for students' mistakes in grammar and spelling? Or do you think there is another reason for these problems?

4 Do you agree that the Internet makes young people want to communicate more? Does it really provide more _____ to write?

5 Is your knowledge of the functions on your mobile phone the same as that of your parents? Or do you know _____ more than they do?

6 Other than Netspeak, what things do young people do these days that parents dislike and _____ about?

VOCABULARY FOCUS 2 | **Knowledge of word roots can be helpful for learning new vocabulary.**

For example:

viv, vit = *life* (<u>vit</u>amin, sur<u>viv</u>e)

trans = *across* (<u>trans</u>port)

transform

vivid

vital

Match the words (1–8) to the correct definitions (a–h).

1	revive	**a**	To move from one place to another
2	vivacious	**b**	Clear or thin enough for you to see things through
3	vital		
4	transfer	**c**	Very important, necessary (important for the life of something)
5	transform	**d**	To change spoken or written words into another language
6	translate		
7	vivid	**e**	Lively and attractive
8	transparent	**f**	To make someone or something completely different
		g	Bring back to life
		h	Very clear and detailed (lifelike)

> **Grammar**
>
> **Not only … but also …**
>
> *Not only … but also …* means *in addition to*.
> The meaning is slightly stronger than just using *and*.
>
> You should **not only** read English well, **but also** speak fluently.
>
> He can type **not only** in English, **but also** in Chinese.

GRAMMAR **Complete the sentences with information about you.**

1 Two things you need to succeed in life.

To succeed in life, I not only have to _____, but I also have to _____.

2 Two things you would like to do before you graduate.

Before I graduate, I would not only like to _____, but I would also like to _____.

3 Two things you can do well.

I can not only _____, but I can also _____.

4 Two things you use your mobile phone or MP3 player for.

I not only use my _____ for _____, but I also use it for _____.

5 Two things your future wife or husband should be.

My future _____ should not only be _____, but also _____.

6 Two things you need to do to get your dream job.

To get my dream job, I not only have to _____, but I also have to _____.

Effective • *Skills*

COMPARING TEXTS Read and compare the emails. With a partner, make a list of all the differences you can find.

For example:

1 *In email A, the student didn't properly greet the professor.*

A

Get Mail Write Contacts Reply Forward Delete Print

I think you made a mistake with my test result. You gave me 24 points, but it should be 25 points. Please check it.

B

Get Mail Write Contacts Reply Forward Delete Print

Hello Professor Anderson,

This is Isabelle Falch from your 11 o'clock English class. I have a question about my test result. You gave me 24 points, but when I checked the numbers, I got a total of 25. Would you mind checking that again? I'm sorry to bother you about this, but I just want to make sure it is correct.

Thank you for your time. I really enjoy your class and I'm glad to have you as my professor.

Formal request email etiquette

For many people, the skill of composing formal emails is extremely important in their academic and professional lives. In formal writing, we expect communication to be polite and respectful, especially when we are asking for something. The following guidelines can help you write polite emails that will leave a good impression and improve your chance of getting a positive reply to your request.

 1 Begin the email by addressing the person politely, using his or her title:

- `Hello Professor Lee`
- `Dear Ms Fletcher`

Only use the person's title with the family name (either the complete name, or just the family name), never with the first name only. Note that when addressing a woman, it is a good idea to always use the Ms title. Mr. and Miss indicate marital status (married or single), and this is considered unnecessary and, to some, offensive in formal situations.

 2 Next, you should identify yourself. Do not assume that the recipient of your email will automatically know who you are:

- `This is Martin Garcia from your 10 o'clock English class.`
- `This is Judit Varga, one of your former English students.`
- `This is Peter Schmidt from Vertex International.`

 3 Before making your request, give the general reason why you are writing:

- `I'm writing about ...`
- `The reason I'm emailing you is ...`

It sounds a little more polite to introduce the topic before making the request. Rushing to make the request too soon can make you seem pushy and inconsiderate.

 4 Next, make your request using polite expressions and sentences, and give the reasons for the request. Try to avoid short and direct request sentences as they can sound rude when writing or speaking to an equal or someone in a higher position than you. Polite expressions are even necessary when addressing someone in a lower position. Here are some examples of requests that are too short and direct:

- `You'd better check my result again.`
- `Let me hand in the homework without a penalty, please.`
- `Please change my mark.`

th@nkyou

All of the above are too short and direct (the first sounds like a threat!). Use longer and more indirect request forms such as the following to make a better impression:

- `Would you mind checking my mark again?`
- `Could you consider sending the documents a little earlier?`
- `Is it possible to change my mark?`
- `Would it be OK if we delayed the meeting for a few days?`

5 After making your request, apologize for any inconvenience the request might make:

- `I'm sorry to have to bother you about this ...`
- `I apologize for any inconvenience this may cause you.`
- `I hope this doesn't cause you too much trouble.`

Even if you feel no need to apologize, just adding these simple words can make you come across as a considerate and respectful person. Remember, the purpose of a request email is to get the person to say yes, not to assign blame or make yourself look good.

6 Finally, thank the reader for considering your request and, if possible, pay some kind of sincere compliment:

- `Thank you for considering my request. I really enjoy your class and I appreciate all the hard work you do.`
- `Thank you for your time. We've really enjoyed working with you and we appreciate all of your help.`

If you cannot think of a sincere compliment, then just finish with the 'thank you' sentence. Compliments that are not sincere or are exaggerated will be seen for what they are: insincere flattery. They could leave the wrong impression.

7 Avoid using informal language like slang and Netspeak. Avoid typing in capital letters. It looks as if you are shouting.

- `You said u did not get my homework, but I DID give it 2 U in class.`

The guidelines above will help you create a good impression which, in turn, makes the recipient more likely to consider your request favourably. While nothing can guarantee a positive response, the above will certainly increase your odds of being successful. Even if the recipient has to reject your request, this type of email will still help you maintain a positive relationship which will be beneficial in future.

IDENTIFYING ERRORS **The emails below do not follow the advice in the text. The type of mistake is numbered. Write the numbers of the mistakes made in each email.**

The author …

1 did not address the recipient correctly.

2 did not identify herself/himself.

3 failed to indicate the topic of the request.

4 did not use appropriate language.

5 did not include an apology.

6 did not thank the reader or pay a sincere compliment.

7 used informal speech or 'shouted'.

A Mistakes: __1__ ___ ___ ___   **B** Mistakes: ___ ___ ___ ___

Get Mail Write Contacts Reply Forward Delete Print	Get Mail Write Contacts Reply Forward Delete Print
Dear Professor John, This is Alfredo from your 2 PM English class. I am writing about the homework that is due today. I am ill today, so I cannot come to class. Please understand me and let me give in my homework on Friday. I am sorry to have to burden you with this request. But I MUST get a good mark, so I don't want to lose points. Thank you for your consideration. I really enjoy your class.	Dear Mr Bronson, I'm afraid that I am very ill today and I won't be able to come to class. Is it possible for this to be an excused absence? I am sorry to make this difficult request to you, but I am very worried about getting an F. I know I haven't been attending class well so far, but I promise I will do my best to attend all classes in future.

WRITING **Write a request to your professor. Follow the advice in the text.**

1 Identify yourself.

2 Give the topic of your request.

3 Make your request.

4 Include an apology sentence.

5 Thank your professor and pay a sincere compliment.

EXERCISE 1

Read the text.

Offline dating: playing it safe

Finding love on the Internet is becoming more and more common in today's fast-paced society. While some people do find love in cyberspace, bear in mind that there are potential dangers. Though most people you meet online may be nice and sincere, there are a few who have bad intentions and some can even be violent. Be very careful about giving out personal information to someone you meet online, such as phone numbers, the name of your workplace, and your address. If you decide to meet in person, make sure you meet in a public place. Also, tell a friend where you are going and who you are going to meet. If possible, give them a photograph of the person you are meeting. If you change locations after you meet, give a make call to your friend to let them know. As they say, it's always better to be safe than sorry.

EXERCISE 2

Correct the sentences so that they agree with the text.

For example:

Not many people try to find love on the Internet.

It is becoming common for people to try to find love on the Internet.

1   Most people who try to find romance through the Internet do not succeed.

2   This advice is to help readers avoid people who are trying to steal their money.

3   Finding romance through the Internet is very dangerous.

4   For the first date, it is good to meet in a quiet, private place.

EXERCISE 3

Match the expressions in **bold** in the sentences to the correct definitions (a–f).

1   We loved each other, but it wasn't **meant to be**. Her family moved to the United States and we lost touch.

2   John tried hard to impress his date, but he **blew it** when he bored her with his army stories.

3   It's hard to **stay upbeat** when the girl of your dreams breaks your heart.

4   I know you are depressed about your boyfriend leaving you, but that was more than a year ago! You have to **get over him**!

5   Why are you so secretive? Why won't you **open up** to me?

6   If you don't **have much in common** with your boyfriend, then what can you do for fun when you are out together?

a   To fail, lose a good opportunity.

b   To share the same interests.

c   Destined, something already decided.

d   To talk freely about your feelings, not be private.

e   To forget about past problems and be happy.

f   To be positive and cheerful.

Review | Unit 6

EXERCISE 1

Read the text and answer the questions in Exercise 2 as quickly as you can. Write your starting and finishing time.

Start time: _____

Finish time: _____

The ever-widening Net

Using the Internet for communication is still very much the realm of the young and the educated. In the United States, 90 per cent of all teenagers between 16–18 and 86 per cent of all college graduates use the Internet regularly. In contrast, only 25 per cent of people over 66 and 33 per cent of adults who did not graduate from high school are online. Those who use Internet technology have formed their own language that outsiders have a hard time understanding. This contributes to a growing communication gap between the young and the elderly, and adds to the growing digital divide between those who have access to computers and those who do not, or who are simply not willing to use them. But as the future belongs to the young, we can expect Internet use to grow and perhaps even replace older forms of communication, such as postal services.

EXERCISE 2

Decide if the sentences are True (T), False (F), or if the information is Not Given (NG) in the text.

1 Using the Internet is becoming increasingly popular with older people.

T ☐   F ☐   NG ☐

2 The more education a person has, the more likely he or she is to use the Internet.

T ☐   F ☐   NG ☐

3 Most adults in the United States do not use the Internet regularly.

T ☐   F ☐   NG ☐

4 The Internet has made it easier for young and elderly people to communicate with each other.

T ☐   F ☐   NG ☐

5 More young people use mobile phones than adults.

T ☐   F ☐   NG ☐

6 Posting letters might not happen in the future.

T ☐   F ☐   NG ☐

7. Language

PRE-READING 1 **Complete the sentences with the key words in bold from the text.**

1 Just being _____ to a new language is not enough to learn it. You need to be able to understand most of what you read and hear.

2 In Quebec, Canada, many people are _____, speaking English and French fluently.

3 Cristina was born in Mexico, so her _____ is Spanish.

4 In this age of globalization, it is a great _____ to speak more than one language.

PRE-READING 2 **Discuss the questions with a partner.**

1 At what age did you first start to study English? Do you wish you had started at an earlier or later age?

2 At what age do you think it is best for children to start learning a second language?

   a from birth

   b 2–5 years old

   c 5–10 years old

   d after the age of 10

PRE-READING 3 **Quickly skim the text by reading the first few sentences of each paragraph. What do you think is the conclusion of the text?**

a It is best to have children start learning a second language as early as possible.

b It is best to wait until children are a little bit older before having them learn a second language.

c What is best for children depends on their environment.

d Researchers and experts still are not sure when is the best time for children to start learning a second language.

Is younger always better?

In this age of globalization, second language skills are more important than ever before. With English skills key to academic and professional success, a growing number of parents in non-English speaking countries have their children begin studying English at the
5 earliest of ages. In countries around the world, pre-schools offering English instruction have become a common sight, and many parents even begin teaching English to their infants. For some educators, the teaching of a foreign language to very young children is a worrying trend. They question whether or not such early introduction of a
10 foreign language will have a harmful effect on the **native language**. Others are convinced that children naturally learn languages better at younger ages, so parents are wise to take advantage of this opportunity.

Will learning a second language too early interfere with the mother
15 tongue? When will second-language instruction be most effective? Is earlier always better? The answers to these questions are not as straightforward as some people believe.

Dr Laura-Ann Petitto, director of the cognitive neuroscience laboratory for language and child development at Dartmouth
20 College, claims it is never too soon for a child to learn a second language. Petitto observed 15 children growing up **bilingual** in a variety of languages, and found there were no substantial differences between the languages they learnt and monolingual users.

'The earlier a child was **exposed** to a second language, the better
25 the child did,' says Petitto. 'This flies in the face of educational policy that suggests exposing a child to only one language at first. A child is not confused by a second language or delayed in learning the community language.' Petitto found that children who first learnt one language, and then began to learn a second, were never quite as
30 good as those who learned both languages simultaneously.

Petitto's findings are consistent with most recent research in the field of bilingualism. There is a good deal of support for the 'critical period': the theory that a child's brain is best suited to learn a language effortlessly and perfectly during the early years. The brain
35 loses this capacity around the onset of puberty (roughly 10–14 years old). Some researchers even claim that as early as the age of five the ability to absorb a new language begins to diminish.

Does this mean that earlier is always better for language learning? Not necessarily. Young children can only take **advantage** of the

40 critical period if they are immersed in an environment that gives sufficient exposure to the language and opportunities for natural interaction over an extended period of time. Successful bilingual children are typically those raised in an environment where the second language is spoken in the community, or within the home
45 where one or both of the parents speak the additional language.

Learning a second language in the classroom, however, is an entirely different matter. Most classrooms cannot give the thousands of hours that are necessary for language learning to take place. Furthermore, classroom settings in Asia rarely provide natural
50 interaction in the language, especially when all the students and even the teacher are non-native speakers of English. Contrary to popular belief, in a classroom setting, younger might actually *not* be better. Several studies have confirmed that, apart from pronunciation skills, older children and early teens learn languages better in the
55 classroom than younger children. Older children generally have superior cognitive skills, attention span, and motivation. These attributes are essential for successful classroom learning.

So what should parents do? If parents can provide a natural environment to develop multiple languages, then this certainly is
60 preferable to having the child learn the language in classrooms at a later age. Although there can be delays in language development for one or both languages, bilingual children typically catch up with their monolingual peers relatively quickly, and can avoid the thousands of hours of language study that students must endure to
65 master a second language as an adult.

But for the majority who are unable to provide the conditions for true bilingual development, then perhaps it is advisable to take a more relaxed and realistic approach to developing second language skills in their children. Many experts recommend that parents give
70 their children regular exposure to a second language through fun songs and videos to help children become accustomed to the rhythm and intonation of the language. Parents can also read to their children to help build up basic vocabulary and give them a sense of how the language is put together. Done regularly, these activities can
75 do much to give a child an advantage by the time he/she begins studying the language at school. However, exposing young children to classroom activities, such as memorizing grammar rules and vocabulary lists, may provide disappointing results. It may also put the children off language learning in the future. And in the long run,
80 that can be far worse than doing nothing at all.

COMPREHENSION 1   **Decide if the sentences are True (T) or False (F). Then write the line number where the evidence is.**

1   Learning a second language too early can harm the development of the first language.

T ☐   F ☐   Line number: _____

2   For children to become a native speaker in two languages, they have to first master one language, and then learn the second.

T ☐   F ☐   Line number: _____

3   In natural learning environments, younger children learn languages best.

T ☐   F ☐   Line number: _____

4   It is not very difficult to provide proper conditions for natural learning of English in classrooms.

T ☐   F ☐   Line number: _____

5   Older children can develop speaking, listening, and pronunciation skills better than younger children in a classroom environment.

T ☐   F ☐   Line number: _____

6   The text implies that teaching young children grammar is not effective.

T ☐   F ☐   Line number: _____

COMPREHENSION 2   **Answer the questions without using a dictionary.**

1   In line 12, what does *take advantage of* mean?

   a   Use an opportunity in a way that will be good for you.

   b   Use something dishonestly for your own benefit.

   c   Take a benefit away from someone else.

2   In line 25, what does *flies in the face of* mean?

   a   attracts attention to

   b   directly opposes

   c   angers or bothers

   d   strongly agrees with

3   In lines 29-30, what does *never quite as good* mean?

   a   always about equal

   b   always a little worse

   c   always much worse

4   In line 30, which word means *at the same time*? _____

5 What is the author's answer to the question in line 38?

   a It is probably true.

   b It is impossible to know if it is true.

   c it could be true in some cases, but could be false in other cases.

   d It is false.

6 In line 41, which word means *opportunities to hear and see*?

   _____

7 In line 66, *majority* refers to …

   a parents.   **b** children.

   c teachers.   **d** linguists.

SPEAKING **Discuss the questions with a partner.**

1 At what age did you begin studying a second language? Did you think the instruction at that time was effective?

2 In the future, if you have children, what might you do for their language education? Circle all that apply.

   a One parent will always speak the second language to the child at home, so the child can grow up in a bilingual environment.

   b I will try to send my child to a foreign country to master the second language.

   c I will read my child stories in the second language and let him/her listen to songs and videos.

   d When my child is three or so, I will send him/her to a pre-school or institute to learn a second language.

   e I will wait until my child is five or six before he/she begins learning a second language at school.

VOCABULARY FOCUS 1 **Complete the sentences with the correct word.**

1 Children moving to foreign countries usually learn the new language perfectly. This seems to _____ the critical period theory.

   a convince   **b** confirm   **c** prefer   **d** diminish

convinced

prefer

2 Good parents are _____ with rules for their children. The rules should generally stay the same, and not change often according to the parents' mood.

   a convincing   **b** preferable   **c** consistent   **d** various

3 At first, I didn't believe that she had mastered three languages, but after hearing her speak, I am now _____.

   a advisable   **b** convinced   **c** confirmed   **d** accustomed

motivation

rush

4 Dr Petitto claims that children have the _____ to learn even *more* than two languages perfectly.

  a consistency b memorization c motivation d capacity

5 Some parents worry that if they _____ English education for their child, the child will never be able to learn English well.

  a delay b stress c rush d expose

6 Playing computer games is fun, but it shouldn't _____ with your school work.

  a delay b relax c expose d interfere

7 In just a few months in Canada, Mrs Lee's son learnt a _____ amount of English.

  a substantial b diminished c consistent d straightforward

8 The longer you go without practising a language, the more your language skills will _____.

  a intervene b delay c diminish d multiply

9 Some children living in Europe don't have any _____ to learn a foreign language. They just can't see why they should learn it.

  a capacity b motivation c interaction d stress

10 It is generally not considered _____ to let very young children learn grammar. The results are usually not so good.

  a wise b consistent c concrete d straightforward

VOCABULARY FOCUS 2

Complete the sentences with the correct word.

1 *confuse/confusion*

  a You can avoid unnecessary _____ in tests if you carefully read the instructions.

  b Be careful though; some teachers try to _____ students with tricky questions.

2 *observed/observation*

  a The principal of the school occasionally _____ teachers teaching their students.

  b From her _____, the principal has discovered that some teachers cannot control their classes well.

3 *prefer/preference*

  a What film would you _____ to see tonight?

  b I don't have any special _____. It's up to you.

4 *interact/interaction*

    a Without sufficient _____ with others, it is difficult to develop communication skills.

    b Students _____ best when the study topic is interesting.

5 *motivate/motivation*

    a A good teacher can _____ his/her students.

    b Without _____, it is hard to do anything well.

6 *intervene/intervention*

    a More and more people call for UN _____ in African countries facing civil war and starvation.

    b The UN, however, is reluctant to _____ in countries undergoing civil war.

Grammar	This comparative structure shows a continuing cause-effect relationship between two actions or conditions.
The ... the ...	the + comparative expression + subject + verb
	A comma always separates the two clauses.
	The more you practise, **the** better you get.
	The earlier a child was exposed to a second language, **the** better the child did.
	The bigger they come, **the** harder they fall.

GRAMMAR 1 **Match the sentence halves to make logical statements.**

1	The more money they earnt	**a**	the healthier you'll be.
2	The longer he waited	**b**	the sooner you will graduate.
3	The longer she studied art	**c**	the more she appreciated it.
4	The harder he studied	**d**	the more they spent.
5	The more classes you take each term	**e**	the better his marks got.
6	The more you exercise	**f**	the angrier he got.

GRAMMAR 2 **Complete the sentences with information about you.**

1 The older I get, the _____.

2 The more I study English, the _____.

3 The more I think about politics these days, the _____.

4 The more technology improves, the _____.

Effective • *Skills*

PREDICTING **Predict the answers to the questions before you read the text.**

1 Which language is spoken by most people in the world?

2 Which language is spoken as a first language in most countries?

3 How many languages are there in the world today?

4 How many languages are expected to exist by the year 2100?

5 Of the following countries, China, India, Indonesia and the United States, which has the most native languages?

6 Which language has the largest vocabulary?

Language *and* the world

Q: Which language is spoken by most people in the world?

A: Mandarin Chinese has the largest number of native speakers, with estimates varying from 800,000 native speakers to nearly a billion. Hindi, Spanish, and English are the next three, though surveys differ in the exact ranking (estimates for each vary from 320,000 to over 500,000).

If the number of people who speak a language as a second or foreign language is included, then English is probably the language that is spoken the most in the world. Language expert, David Crystal estimates that a total of 1.4 billion people speak English as a native or foreign language, with the total number of people able to speak Mandarin Chinese around 1.2 billion. This might not last for long, though, as Chinese is becoming an increasingly popular foreign language for study in many countries.

Q and A

Q: Which language is spoken as a first language in most countries?

A: No language is spoken as a mother tongue in more countries than Spanish. A total of 22 countries claim Spanish as their official or co-official language, most of them in Central and Latin America. Spanish is not an official language in the United States, but it has 31 million Spanish-speaking citizens and this number is expected to grow.

Q: How many languages are there in the world today? How many languages are expected to exist by the year 2100?

A: Experts estimate 6,000–6,800 languages are currently spoken in the world, but this number is decreasing rapidly. Some experts believe that languages are dying out at a rate of one language every two weeks, while others estimate the loss is one per month. At this rate, about half of the currently existing languages will disappear in this century. Some experts have more pessimistic predictions, as they believe the rate of language loss will only increase. The growth of English has some effect on this dwindling number of languages, but Spanish, Portuguese, Russian, Arabic, and Chinese have each replaced just as many if not more local languages in various parts of the world. Already, 4–5 per cent of all the world's languages are spoken by over 90 per cent of the world's population, and half of the world speaks one of the ten most common languages. Linguists call for more awareness of language preservation and the benefits of bilingualism, and also stronger efforts by governments and communities to maintain native tongues.

Q: Which of the following countries has the most native languages: China, India, Indonesia or the United States?

A: Although all of the above countries have numerous native languages spoken within their borders, none of them comes close to Indonesia. Indonesia has a population of 230 million people speaking an estimated 742 native languages spread across more than 17,000 islands. The official language taught in schools and used in the media is Bahasa Indonesian. However, there is another country with even more languages than Indonesia. Papua New Guinea is home to over 800 different languages, more than 10 per cent of all of the world's languages! Nigeria follows Indonesia with 516, followed by India with 427, and the United States with 311. The majority of these languages are expected to die out within the next century.

Q: Which language has the largest vocabulary?

A: Language experts say it is impossible to make a very reliable estimate of how many words a language has. Historically, English has had a lot of contact with and been influenced by speakers of many other languages, and thus is probably larger in comparison to other languages. The *Oxford English Dictionary* contains over 170,000 words that are currently in use. Add to this current slang and colloquial expressions, and the number would be much higher. Don't worry, no one expects you to learn that many words! The average native speaker of English only knows a fraction of these, 18,000–40,000 by some estimates. Some language experts suggest that a learner of English needs only around 10,000 words to become an advanced speaker, and even a strong knowledge of just the most common 2,000–3,000 words can be enough for basic, but effective, communication and comprehension.

QandA

COMPREHENSION   Check your answers to the Predicting exercise on page 79.

INFERRING   **Which of the following inferences can you logically make from the text?**

1   By the year 2200, there might be fewer than 1,500 languages in the world.

2   In the future, Spanish will be the official language in the United States.

3   Mandarin Chinese may soon be the most widely spoken language in the world (as a first or second language).

4   Many Indonesians speak at least two languages.

5   Many governments are making efforts to save minority languages in their countries.

6   More than 20 per cent of all the world's languages can be found in South-East Asia.

7   It is common for societies to borrow words from other cultures they come into contact with.

8   You need to know 10,000 English words before you can speak with a native English speaker.

8 • Populations in peril

PRE-READING 1 **Complete the sentences with the key words in bold from the text.**

1 After graduating from university, most students will get jobs and join the _____ of the country.

2 The number of panda bears began _____ in 1949. Today, there are only 1,000–3,000 panda bears alive.

3 High _____ in some countries have led to large increases in population.

4 Most _____ in the United States are from Asia or Latin America.

PRE-READING 2 **Discuss the questions with a partner.**

1 How many children would you like to have?

2 What are some of the reasons why couples these days do not have many children?

PRE-READING 3 **Quickly scan the text to find the information.**

1 When will the population of the Earth reach 7 billion?

2 What specific countries are discussed in this reading?

3 How much money does it cost to educate a child in Korea?

4 Which is the second largest racial/ethnic group in the United States?

Endangered populations

As of 2006, there are an estimated 6.5 billion people on the planet and by 2012 this number will reach 7 billion. For decades, alarmists have warned of an overpopulated world with insufficient resources and indeed this threat remains. It is ironic,
5   then, that for more and more developed countries the main demographic challenge is not overpopulation, but a **declining** one. Though the reasons for falling birth rates vary from country to country, all countries with declining populations face similar social and economic consequences.

10   Russia and 16 other countries that were formerly a part of the Soviet Union have seen their populations shrink over the past decade. As of 2004, there are 5 million fewer Russians on the planet than in 1992, and the numbers continue to drop by 700,000–800,000 each year. In addition to health-care issues,
15   Moscow-based journalist Oleg Glebov claims the overall state of depression following the breakup of the Soviet Union is a key factor in the declining population. 'Most people are very pessimistic. They don't believe children will have a future.'

Things may not be so gloomy in western Europe, but nonetheless
20   couples are still reluctant to have children, with Germany, Spain, and Italy having the lowest birth rates in all of Europe. Rising levels of education and prosperity, increased female presence in the workforce, and birth control are the leading causes of low **birth rates** in western Europe. An EU survey asked couples
25   how many children they wanted to have in the future, and the average was 2.36, roughly one more child than European women are actually having. This may be due in part to some European women having fewer children due to the difficulties of pregnancy and child-raising. Concerns over losing their position in the
30   workplace and thus struggling financially may also be a factor.

Asian countries have some of the lowest birth rates in the world. They share the same reasons for this phenomenon as western Europe, but unique to Asia is the reluctance of families to have more than one or two children due to the steadily rising price of
35   education. The cost of supporting a child from birth to graduation in Japan and Korea is estimated to be about US $128,000. In Korea, many families spend half of their total income on education alone. Japan's population has been declining and if current trends continue, the population is estimated to fall by 20 per
40   cent by the year 2035, and could be half of what it is now within a hundred years. Korea is not far behind. In 2005, Korea took the

dubious honour of attaining the lowest birth rate in the world at 1.08 and is expected to reach zero population growth in 2020.

Countries with low birth rates become aging societies with a
45 workforce that is unable to keep the economy growing and support the elderly. The consequences are weakened economies, labour shortages, deep cuts in social programmes, and much higher taxes for those in the workforce. In Italy and Germany, 20 per cent of the population is over 65 and this percentage is expected to double
50 in the next 25 years. In Japan, there are already more people over the age of 65 than under the age of 15. By the year 2050, in many developed countries, the proportion of elderly citizens to those in the workforce may be an unimaginable ratio of 1:1.

Immigration is one way to replenish a **workforce**, but this is
55 not always an easy solution. Immigration has helped the United States maintain a healthy economy despite a low birth rate among the majority race, white Americans. The trade-off is a radical change in the racial and cultural make-up of the society. As non-Hispanic, white Americans continue to have fewer and fewer
60 children, immigrant minority numbers are rising rapidly. By 2050, white Americans will still be the largest racial group, but they will make up less than half of the total American population. The fastest growing minority is Hispanic, which currently makes up slightly over 14 per cent of the population, surpassing the African-
65 American population in 2000. Already, Hispanics are the majority race in Los Angeles, and will be the dominant racial/ethnic group in California and Texas in the next few decades. Some feel that as the United States has always been a nation of **immigrants**, this kind of change is no great cause for concern. Whether or not the
70 traditionally homogeneous countries of Asia and Europe will be able to tolerate such fundamental changes in the racial and cultural make-up of their societies may be another matter, however.

In the meantime, European and Asian governments promote ambitious programmes to encourage couples to have more
75 children, but declining populations have proven very difficult to reverse. Thus far, no country that has fallen below a birth rate of 1.5 has managed to rise back to the population replacement level of 2.1. Robert Retherford of the East West Center states that the dilemma for governments is finding ways of keeping the economy
80 competitive in the global marketplace while making societies more marriage friendly, particularly in regard to married women in the workforce. Says Retherford, 'It won't be easy and it won't be cheap.'

COMPREHENSION 1 **Decide if the sentences are True (T) or False (F). Then write the line number where the evidence is.**

1 Overpopulation is no longer a problem.

T ☐   F ☐   Line number: _____

2 Many western Europeans do not have children because of health problems and lack of hope for the future.

T ☐   F ☐   Line number: _____

3 The text implies that social and economic improvements in a society can lead to lower birth rates.

T ☐   F ☐   Line number: _____

4 Some of the reasons for the low birth rate in Korea and Japan are rising levels of education, and more women working.

T ☐   F ☐   Line number: _____

5 If current trends continue, the Korean race will begin to decline after 2020.

T ☐   F ☐   Line number: _____

6 If current population trends continue, Hispanics will be the majority racial/ethnic group in the United States by 2050.

T ☐   F ☐   Line number: _____

7 The author believes that immigration is a simple solution to the population problems of developed countries.

T ☐   F ☐   Line number: _____

8 We can infer that the author is optimistic about developed countries solving their population problems.

T ☐   F ☐   Line number: _____

COMPREHENSION 2 **Complete the table with information from the text.**

	Reasons for low birth rate	Effects of low birth rate
Russia		
Western Europe		
Korea, Japan		

COMPREHENSION 3   **Answer the questions without using a dictionary.**

1   In lines 5–10, which word means *decreasing* (to become less in number or size)?

    _____

2   In line 19, which word means *sad, with little hope*?

    _____

3   In line 42, what does the expression *dubious honour* mean?

    a   Though normally it is respectable to be number one in something, it is not really respectable in this case.

    b   Though this situation is not a good thing generally, it is still respectable.

    c   There are both good and bad aspects of being number one in this case.

4   In line 43, what does *zero population growth* mean?

    a   The population will be reduced to zero.

    b   The population will grow at a constant rate.

    c   The population will stop growing at this time.

5   In line 53, what is implied by the word *unimaginable*?

    a   The writer finds the situation shocking and alarming.

    b   The writer finds the situation exciting.

    c   The writer finds the situation too difficult to understand.

6   In line 57, which word or expression means *you gain one thing, but have to lose another thing*? _____

7   Re-read lines 69-72. What is implied by *may be another matter*?

    a   This would be an additional cause of population decrease.

    b   This situation might not be a problem in European countries.

    c   European countries might have trouble dealing with large immigrant populations.

8   In line 73, what is the meaning of *In the meantime*?

    a   during these difficult times

    b   for now; at this time

    c   for the future

SPEAKING **Which of these ideas do you agree with? Put them in order of effectiveness. Discuss your answers with a partner.**

- [ ] increased immigration
- [ ] higher taxes for people with no children
- [ ] lower taxes for large families
- [ ] financial rewards for having more than one child
- [ ] a reduction in education costs
- [ ] forcing companies to provide better childcare facilities
- [ ] delaying retirement age
- [ ] other _____

VOCABULARY FOCUS 1 **Complete the summary with the words in the box.**

declining	citizens	proportion	immigration	encourage
reverse	elderly	estimated	decrease	replenish

Many people typically worry about overpopulation, but in some countries population growth is (**1**)_____. In these countries, the number of (**2**)_____ people is growing, with fewer young people to support them. For example, in Japan, the (**3**)_____ of elderly people to young workers is about 1:4. No one knows for sure, but it is (**4**)_____ that the population of Japan will (**5**)_____ by 50 per cent over the next 100 years.

Governments hope to (**6**)_____ this trend, and get birth rates above 2.0, the rate needed to (**7**)_____ the population. Some governments (**8**)_____ their (**9**)_____ to have more children. Others believe that encouraging more (**10**)_____ is the way to solve the problem.

VOCABULARY FOCUS 2 <u>Underline</u> **the word that does not belong in each group.**

For example:

	nice	pleasant	<u>terrible</u>	fantastic
1	sufficient	lacking	enough	adequate
2	former	previous	current	before
3	temporarily	steadily	continually	non-stop
4	decline	shrink	maintain	drop
5	honour	disgrace	insult	shame
6	consequence	result	cause	effect

sufficient

non-stop

consequence

disgrace

<table>
<tr><td>**Grammar**</td><td>The choice of present simple or present perfect depends on what time frame we focus on.</td></tr>
<tr><td>**Present simple and present perfect**</td><td>**a** The information is simply factual with no focus on any particular time.
*Population decline **is** always a concern for governments.*

b Focus on the current situation only.
*The low birth rate **is** a problem for Europe these days.*

c Focus simultaneously on the present and the past.
*The low birth rate **has been** a problem for several years.*

Another use of the present perfect is to indicate or ask about some activity that has happened before in the indefinite past.
*I **have gone** bungee jumping before.* ***Have** you ever **seen** a ghost?*</td></tr>
</table>

GRAMMAR 1   **Read sentences 1–8 and identify the function of the verb form. Choose from a–d.**

1 Elizabeth has always been a good worker. _____

2 She doesn't work now, though. _____

3 Hans studies hard for the IELTS test. _____

4 He has attended an English institute for the past four months. _____

5 He hasn't taken the test yet, though. _____

6 The term *pollution* refers to any substances that have a harmful effect on air, water, or land. _____

7 Many countries have serious problems with pollution. _____

8 We have never had such serious problems before. _____

a No specific time focus. States a general fact that is always true.

b Only tells us about the present situation.

c Tells us the action or situation is happening now, and for how long it has happened.

d Tells us an event has happened before in the indefinite past, or has never happened before.

GRAMMAR 2   **Tick (✔) the sentences that are true for you. Discuss your answers with a partner.**

☐ I have a boyfriend/girlfriend.

☐ I have had a boyfriend/girlfriend for _____ months.

☐ I live with my parents.

☐ I live away from my parents.

☐ I have lived away from my parents for _____.

☐ I have never lived away from my parents.

☐ I have a part-time job.

☐ I don't have a part-time job right now.

☐ I have never had a part-time job.

Effective • *Skills*

Why do some people choose not to get married? Brainstorm a list of reasons with a partner. Read the text to see if the reasons you mentioned are included.

A happy, married life?

NO, THANK YOU!

Most people dream of a beautiful wedding ceremony with their Mr or Mrs Right. They imagine a harmonious family with two lovely children enjoying a home-cooked dinner every evening. That is the typical image of a happy married life and it is believed that everybody needs a family to provide love, rest, and contentment. However, ever since I was a young girl, I have had a different point of view about marriage. Marriage is just an option, and in my case, the word 'marriage' is not in my dictionary. Marriage does not guarantee love and it will require me to accept difficult roles that I do not wish to have.

The idea that marriage ensures long-lasting love and happiness is just an illusion. People say that marriage is a symbol of love and commitment. However, many happy couples live together without being married. Further,

5

10

15

20

25

25 domestic violence in the family is reported daily and 4 out of 10 couples divorce within three years of their wedding ceremony. Where are the holy marriage vows that they made before? Yet despite the rising frequency of divorce, being divorced is regarded as a sign of failure in society and thus there is pressure to stay in bad, even abusive relationships. Furthermore, even today when couples divorce, women are far more likely than men to
30 face the responsibility of child-rearing.

I do not want to be under the pressure of a legal commitment. Love should be truly honest, and we cannot be forced to sustain this feeling. It is very natural that the feeling of love comes and goes. Men and women should
35 make an effort to deepen their love, but should break up if they find there is no longer any happiness in their relationship. People pursue love to be happy, and if they are happy in their love, it does not matter whether they are married or not. Marriage itself is just a piece of paper and nothing more.

Married women suffer more hardship and pressure in the workplace
40 and home. Society requires a great deal of sacrifice from women. People complain that the low birth rate is a big social problem and children feel neglected because two-career couples are increasing. Maybe so, but childcare costs can be very high, and it is all too often women, not men, who end up taking care of the children. In addition, many men believe
45 that women should work outside the home as well as doing most of the housework. Modern society expects us to be superwomen.

I do not want to be this kind of exhausted and unappreciated person. In my life, the most important things are me and my career. I am goal-oriented
50 and ambitious, and I have been studying and working hard to attain my dreams. To be honest, I am not self-sacrificing enough to accept the roles that are imposed on a wife and mother. When I have free time, I want to meet friends, pursue hobbies, read books and study, so there will be no time to rear kids and do housework. Marriage cannot satisfy what I would like to achieve and what I am looking for in life. Some people might say that I am
55 too young to understand how important marriage is, or that I am a radical feminist who rejects social convention. But I am what I am, and I do not need to change myself and what I want to have, just because of unfair social expectations and demands. I can be happy, successful, and enjoy my life without marriage.

Read the outline of an essay.

Thesis: *Marriage does not guarantee love and it will require me to accept difficult roles that I do not wish to have.*

Main argument A:
Marriage does not guarantee a happy life or lasting love.

Main argument B:
Married women suffer from unfair demands made on them.

Which argument (A or B) do these sentences support?

☐ Married women sacrifice a lot, but are not respected in society.

☐ Society looks down on you if you get divorced.

☐ It's possible to love someone without being married.

☐ The divorce rate is high.

☐ Companies do not provide enough assistance to married women.

☐ Marriage puts pressure on people who are not in love to stay together.

☐ Men expect women to have a career and take care of the house.

☐ Marriage forces women to abandon their career goals and hobbies.

DISCUSSION **Discuss the questions with a partner.**

1 What is your reaction to the essay? Review the outline above. Which points do you agree with? Which points do you disagree with?

2 Do you feel you could be satisfied with life if you never got married? Why?/Why not?

3 What expectations do you have for your future spouse about earning money?

   a He/She should completely support our family.

   b He/She should provide about half of our family income.

   c He/She should only provide a small portion of the income.

   d He/She does not have to provide any income.

4 What expectations do you have of your future spouse with regard to housework and taking care of children?

   a He/She should do almost all the work at home.

   b He/She should do most of the work at home.

   c He/She should do about half of the work at home.

   d He/She should do just a little.

   e He/She shouldn't do any work at home.

EXERCISE 1

Read the text and answer the questions in Exercise 2 as quickly as you can. Write your starting and finishing time.

Start time: _____

Finish time: _____

Language learning: a matter of time

The Foreign Service Institute (FSI) has been teaching government officials in the United States world languages for more than 55 years. In a recent report on language learning, the FSI concluded that the single most important factor in learning a language is time. 'There is no substitute for simply spending time using the language. Our experience at FSI indicates unequivocally that the amount of time spent in reading, listening to, and interacting in the language has a close relationship to the learner's ability to learn to use that language professionally.' Just how much time is necessary to learn a language depends on how similar or different the new language is to the student's mother tongue. According to FSI data, native English speakers can become competent in languages closely related to English like Spanish, French and Norwegian after 600 hours of instruction and practice, but need at least 800 hours of quality exposure to learn languages such as Greek, Hindi, and Russian. Finally, they need 2,200 hours of instruction and practice to learn a language like Arabic, Chinese, or Japanese. Those numbers are probably similar for people in these countries learning the English language. So if you really want to learn a language well, the first thing you have to do is make a commitment to put in a lot of time.

EXERCISE 2

Decide if the sentences are True (T), False (F), or if the information is Not Given (NG) in the text.

1 Nothing is more important in learning a language than a willingness to spend time seeing, hearing, and practising the language.

T ☐   F ☐   NG ☐

2 A native English speaker learning Japanese needs to study twice as long as a native English speaker studying Spanish.

T ☐   F ☐   NG ☐

3 Students with a high IQ can learn languages more quickly than other students.

T ☐   F ☐   NG ☐

4 People from the Middle East probably need about 2,200 hours of instruction to become competent in English.

T ☐   F ☐   NG ☐

5 Arabic and Asian languages have become more important to learn in the United States in recent years.

T ☐   F ☐   NG ☐

6 The reading infers that Japanese students can learn another Asian language like Korean in about 600 hours.

T ☐   F ☐   NG ☐

EXERCISE 1

Read the text.

Our shrinking planet

Although birth rates have declined in some countries, the world population continues to **boom**. Between 1800 and 1927, the population of the world doubled to 2 billion, and then doubled again in less than 50 years. As of 2005, the world's population is about 6.4 billion and increasing annually by roughly 77 million. **Analysts** are concerned about the additional strain population growth will put on the world's resources, particularly with regard to water and food. According to the UN World Water Development Report in 2003, severe water **shortages** will affect the majority of the planet within the next 50 years, which will have a strong effect on agriculture and thus the world's food supply. Most of the world's population growth is taking place in developing countries, and it is these regions that can expect to be hit the hardest by **famine** in the years to come.

EXERCISE 2

Answer the questions.

1 What is the main problem discussed in the text?

2 What was the population of the world in 1800?

3 About when did the world's population increase to 4 billion people?

4 What are analysts concerned about?

5 What major problems might people face in the future?

6 Which areas of the world can expect to suffer most from these problems?

EXERCISE 3

Match the key words in bold in the text to the correct definitions (1–4).

1 A serious lack of food that causes many people to become ill or die

_____

2 To grow or develop quickly

_____

3 A lack of something that you need or want

_____

4 Someone whose job is to carefully examine a situation in order to provide other people with information

_____

9• Sports

PRE-READING 1 **Discuss the questions with a partner.**

1 What are the most popular sports in your country? Which do you enjoy watching and playing?

2 Did you watch the last World Cup? If so, what were your best (and worst) memories of the games?

PRE-READING 2 **Match the words (1–5) to their definitions (a–e).**

1 elimination

2 tournament

3 parity

4 domination

5 ranking

a A series of games in which the winner of each game plays in the next game, until there is one player or team left.

b Control or power over people or things.

c A situation in which different people or things are equal.

d A position on a list that shows how good someone is compared to others.

e The process of removing someone from a competition.

PRE-READING 3 **Skim the text and write the number of each paragraph next to its topic.**

For example:

☐3☐ World Cup football and national passion.

☐ Excess of popular sports in the United States.

☐ Popularity of World Cup football in general.

☐ Looking forward to the 2010 games.

☐ Explanation for World Cup football popularity.

☐ Historical reasons why many North Americans might not be interested in football.

The greatest show on earth

No sports event, or perhaps any single event for that matter, comes even close to World Cup football on the global stage. As has happened for decades, much of the world again stopped dead in its tracks to watch the 2006 World Cup hosted by Germany. For over a billion people, offices closed, university classes were cancelled, and if your country happened to be half a planet away from Germany, nearly the entire nation woke up at 4am just to watch 22 men chase a ball around a field.

What are the reasons for football's strong appeal to people from so many different cultures and backgrounds? For one thing, football gives all nations a degree of parity that is not always found in other sports. 'Football's universality is its simplicity—the fact that the game can be played anywhere with anything,' says *National Geographic* writer Sean Wilsey. Rich or poor, all countries from all climates have equal access to the sport, which needs very little equipment to play. It is also a game in which spirit, determination, and creativity are just as important as physical characteristics, giving no particular race any clear advantage. Indeed, players from regions all over the world have entered and made an impact on the top European football leagues. Football is a game where upsets can and often do happen. Once the World Cup starts, it is certain that some of the football powerhouses will stumble and a few underdogs will move on to the single elimination rounds. In the 2006 World Cup, five of the 16 teams to go on to the elimination rounds were not ranked among the top 20 teams before the tournament began. Every team having a fighting chance just adds to the excitement.

For many people, the attraction of football goes even deeper than just sport. Trinidadian historian C L R James recognized sport as a form of ritualized combat, stirring national passion in ways that are second only to war. Games between rivals such as Germany and the Netherlands, France and Italy, and Brazil and Argentina can bring the level of intensity among fans to a fever pitch, often with violent results. Perhaps no other sport can bring out both the passion and ugliness in humanity as football, evidenced by the ecstatic celebrations when your country's team comes out on top, and the riots that can break out when the calls go against your team. This is only amplified when countries with historical and political tensions meet on the football field. Whenever England has played Argentina since the 1980s, it is as if the fans of both countries relive the Falklands/Malvinas War. When Korea or China faces off with Japan, for many, the previous century of conflict is re-enacted on the field.

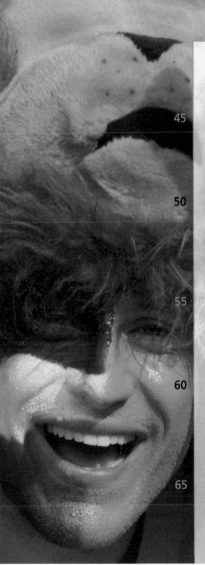

So while football is truly the world's game, it is odd that one of the very few countries not to take to football is the United States. There is no shortage of theories on why most North Americans have such
45   little interest in a sport that is so loved by the rest of the world. Some suggest historical reasons. 'North America was all about being independent from Great Britain, so football's inability to stick here really is a product of historical forces,' says Purdue University historian Randy Roberts. *Irish Times* writer Paddy Agnew agrees that
50   the early rejection of football in North American society was, 'As much to do with declaring independence from England as anything else. Your sports are your identity.'

This hardly explains the continued lack of interest not only in the United States, but in Canada as well, however. Perhaps a more
55   persuasive reason is that North America is already dominated by baseball, basketball, hockey and American football. Boxing, car racing, golf, tennis and figure skating also enjoy relatively high levels of popularity. With so many sports already competing for the public's attention in the United States, there seems to be little time or energy
60   left for other professional sports, especially for one in which neither the United States nor Canada have traditionally excelled.

And yet, with or without North America's blessing, the 'beautiful game' will merrily go on. People are already talking about 2010 when the games will be hosted by South Africa. Will Italy be able
65   to repeat as champions, as they did back in the 1930s? Will Brazil come back to dominate? Will playing the games in Africa give African teams a psychological boost that comes from the home field advantage? Which teams will surprise? Which teams will disappoint? It should be another great show.

COMPREHENSION 1   **Each sentence in the summary has one mistake. <u>Underline</u> and correct the wrong information. The first one has been done for you as an example.**

(1) Football is the most popular sport in <u>the United States</u>, as evidenced by yet another successful World Cup. (2) One reason for football's popularity is that few countries have a chance to succeed in the sport. (3) Football also lessens feelings of nationalism. (4) Matches between countries with historical conflicts become less important to the countries involved. (5) The United States is one of the many countries in which football is not popular. (6) Some suggest it is due to historical conflicts between Europe and North America. (7) Another reason is that the United States and Mexico already have too many popular sports competing for people's attention. (8) Nonetheless, World Cup football will continue to be the world's game, and many people are looking forward to the 2008 World Cup in South Africa.

COMPREHENSION 2   **Answer the questions without using a dictionary.**

1   In lines 3–4, what does *stopped dead in its tracks* mean?

    a   stop briefly   **b**   stop completely   **c**   stop and suffer

2   In line 11, what does *a degree of parity* mean?

    a   equal to some extent   **b**   somewhat different   **c**   highly competitive

3   In line ___, what does the word *upset* mean?

    a   an illness that affects the stomach

    b   an occasion when someone defeats an opponent who is considered better than them

    c   something that makes you feel worried or angry

4   In lines 21 and 22, what do *powerhouses* and *underdogs* mean?

    a   physically strong teams and small and quick teams

    b   teams expected to win and teams not expected to win

    c   teams that play with power and teams that play unfairly

5   In line 22, which word means *fail*?

    _____

6   What is the message of lines 28–30?

    a   Sport is much like a symbolic war that excites nationalism.

    b   Sport can lead to war-like violence.

    c   Sport is good for its ability to bring a country together.

7   In line 44, what does *no shortage of theories* mean?

    a   There are no simple and easy theories.

    b   There are many theories.

    c   There is no time to list all the theories.

8   In lines 47–48, which expression means *cannot become successful*?

    _____

SPEAKING   **Discuss the questions with a partner.**

1   Generally, which national teams do you favour in the World Cup? Who do you think will win the next World Cup?

2   What are some of the bad points of World Cup football? What would you like to see changed?

3   What are some popular sports in other countries that are not popular in your country?

VOCABULARY FOCUS 1

Complete the text with the words in the box.

participated	held	dominated	host
eliminating	appeal	advantage	competing

In 1991, the first FIFA Women's World Cup was (**1**)_____ in China. 12 teams from around the world (**2**)_____, with the United States defeating Norway in the championship game. Norway got their revenge in the 1995 World Cup, however, (**3**)_____ the US team in the semi-finals before beating Germany in the final match. Germany has (**4**)_____ recently, winning the last two World Cup competitions in 2003 and 2007. Germany will also have the home field (**5**) _____ when they (**6**)_____ the 2011 World Cup. As of yet, women's football does not have the same (**7**)_____ as men's football, but its popularity is growing, with more and more young women (**8**)_____ in football leagues around the world each year.

VOCABULARY FOCUS 2

Use the words in the box to label the picture.

save	shoot	tackle	throw-in	dribble	head	score
penalty spot	forward	goal	goal post	crossbar	referee	
penalty area	goalkeeper	strikers	defenders	midfielders		

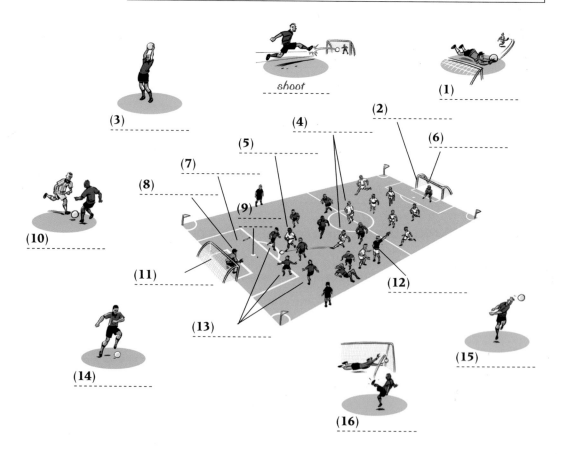

VOCABULARY FOCUS 3

Match the words in **bold** in the sentences to the correct definitions (a–f).

1   We've made our final proposal, so now **the ball's in your court**. Are you going to accept it, or not?

2   Why do you think someone as smart and beautiful as Rachelle would date someone like you? She's way **out of your league**.

3   You really should be careful about making the professor angry. I've tried to get a book published for five years now, but with no results. Maybe it's time to **throw in the towel** and try something else.

4   You have to be ready to **play hard ball** when it comes to business. Being nice isn't going to get you what you want.

5   At school, we only had to memorize grammar rules and vocabulary in English. But it's **a whole new ball game** at the top universities, as they expect you to be able to speak and write in English, as well.

6   Our company's survival depends on this project, so let's make sure we don't **drop the ball** on this one.

a   To use any methods to defeat someone, even unfair or dishonest ones.

b   When it is up to you to make a decision or take the next step.

c   To be unsuccessful in trying to do something.

d   A situation that is completely different from what has happened before.

e   To give up when you know you are going to lose.

f   Beyond one's ability; too good or difficult for someone.

Grammar	*With* phrases are very useful for giving information which provides a context for the main part of the sentence. They are often used at the beginning of sentences.
With phrases	***With so many sports already competing for the public's attention in North America**, there seems to be little time or energy left for other professional sports.*
	***With winter coming soon**, people are beginning to worry about oil shortages.*

GRAMMAR 1   **Match the sentence halves to make logical statements.**

1   With more African athletes playing in the top European leagues,

2   With so much money involved in the World Cup,

3   With the home field advantage,

4   With more and more questionable calls from referees,

5   With so many players intentionally diving,

6   With the problems of violence among football fans,

a   some people are suggesting that FIFA use instant-replay technology to change bad calls.

b   teams can play better thanks to the support of their fans.

c   people question the sportsmanship of today's football players.

d   FIFA has asked for increased security at games.

e   African national teams are becoming more competitive.

f   advertisers can make a lot of money through sponsoring World Cup football.

GRAMMAR 2   **Complete the sentences with information about you.**

1   With language skills so important in the world today, _____.

2   With all the tests and homework I have, _____.

3   With oil prices rising higher and higher, _____.

4   With traffic being so bad in the city, _____.

5   With the weather we've been having lately, _____.

6   With all the work we have done in this class so far, _____.

Effective • *Skills*

DISCUSSION **Discuss the questions with a partner.**

1 In every sporting event, there are always some calls by referees that people question. What are some of the worst referee calls you have seen in major sporting events?

2 What can be done to prevent poor referee decisions from interfering with games?

INCREASING READING SPEED **Try to read the text a little faster than you normally read. Record your time.**

Start time: _____

Finish time: _____

A slight case of **sunstroke**

I was a visitor in Perivia. It was the day of the annual football match between Perivia and Panagura. More than a hundred thousand fans were going to the game. I didn't want to go to watch it.

My friend told me about last year's match. It sounded more like a battle than
5 a game of football. Perivia had lost the match. The Perivians said the referee had not done his job properly.
'Why didn't you give the referee a bribe?' I asked.
'We did,' my friend replied. 'We gave him a lot of money. But the Panagurans gave him much more.'

10 I changed my mind. I went to the match with my friend. The stadium was full of people. The police searched everyone.
The search at the entrance took a long time. The police were looking for dangerous weapons. I bought a programme. It was large, with a silver cover, and it was called the Special Victory Souvenir Issue.

15 How do the Perivians know that they are going to win? I wondered.
I began to read my programme. Among other things, it said that the fifty thousand Perivian soldiers in the stadium had free copies of the programme. Who paid for those fifty thousand copies? I thought.

At last the game began. After half a minute, one of the Perivian players
20 tripped up a Panaguran and the Panaguran fell to the ground. The referee did

nothing. This time, I thought to myself, the Perivians have paid a big enough bribe to the referee.

The players moved quickly down the field and the referee ran after them. He was running slowly. Suddenly, I understood what was wrong. Have you ever seen a man trying to run when he is wearing a bullet-proof vest? I can tell you, it isn't easy! I began to feel sorry for the referee.

The game went peacefully for a time. I began to feel disappointed. Then there was a fight between five players. A few minutes later, four of them were carried off the field.

When the game started again, the Panagurans immediately scored a goal. The crowd roared with rage. A moment later, the referee gave the Panagurans a free kick at goal. They scored: two nil to the Panagurans.

After the first angry roar, the crowd became very still. The silence was frightening. I felt very sorry for that referee. At that moment, he was the most hated man in all Perivia.

A few seconds before half-time, Perivia scored a beautiful goal. The referee blew the whistle. I couldn't believe what had happened. The referee had not allowed the goal. The crowd went mad. At last, the police calmed them down. The two teams moved back to their own sides of the field. The referee stood all alone in the middle of the field.

I heard the sound of a bugle blowing. Then I heard it again. All at once, the crowd seemed to disappear in a sea of fire. The blinding light hurt my eyes. For a moment, I thought there had been an explosion.

I opened my eyes and looked up. Everything was exactly the same, except for one thing. One man had disappeared. There had been a referee in the middle of that football field. Now, there was only a small pile of smoking ashes.

What had happened? I turned to my friend. He was shocked, too. But he was looking down at the silver-coloured programme on his knee. And then I understood.

There is a lot of power in sunlight. A lot of heat can be reflected from a square of silver. At the sound of the bugle, those fifty thousand soldiers in the crowd had lifted up their programmes. Each programme had reflected the rays of the sun. They had reflected the rays of the sun at the referee. The heat had burned him to ashes.

Another referee came onto the football field. He did his job properly and the game ended peacefully. The score was 14–2 to Perivia. No one seemed sorry for the dead referee. In Perivia, football is a serious business.

COMPREHENSION   **Decide if the sentences are True (T) or False (F).**

1   In the previous year, Perivia lost the football match because they did not give money to the referee.

T ☐   F ☐

2   This year the game is held in Perivia.

T ☐   F ☐

3   The narrator probably went to the game because he loves football.

T ☐   F ☐

4   The police searched all the fans because they were worried about violence.

T ☐   F ☐

5   The referee moved slowly because he was hurt.

T ☐   F ☐

6   The referee was probably bribed by Panagurans.

T ☐   F ☐

7   The referee died from gunshot wounds.

T ☐   F ☐

8   The Perivian soldiers were responsible for the referee's death.

T ☐   F ☐

SUMMARY COMPLETION   **Complete the summary with the words in the box.**

Panagura	ashes	intense	Perivia	
bullet-proof	was making	soldiers		bugle
reflected	referee	programmes		bribed

Every year Perivia and Panagura have a football match. Last year, (**1**)_____ won because they gave the referee more money. This year, it seemed that the referee had also been (**2**)_____ by Panagura because he (**3**)_____ bad calls against Perivia. He moved slowly because he was wearing a (**4**)_____ vest. After a very poor call against (**5**)_____, the referee was standing alone in the centre of the field. A (**6**)_____ sounded twice, and then all the (**7**)_____ lifted up their (**8**)_____ and (**9**)_____ sunlight on the referee. The heat was so (**10**)_____ that he was reduced to (**11**)_____. A new (**12**)_____ came on the field and Perivia went on to win the game.

10· Overcoming stereotypes

Complete the sentences with the key words in bold from the text.

1 By _____, newly hatched sea turtles travel overland in the direction of the sea.

2 The United States and Canada have many _____ groups. For example, there are large numbers of black, Hispanic, Asian, and, of course, white Caucasians living there.

3 Students in their first year of university have a _____ to drink too much and neglect their studies.

4 In my travels, I have realized that most of the _____ of Muslims do not accurately describe them.

Complete the following sentences with one of the words from the box to make the statement true for you. Discuss the questions with a partner.

Almost all	Most	Some	Few	None

1 _____ of my friends are not from my home country.

2 _____ of my friends have different religious beliefs to mine.

3 _____ of my friends have negative attitudes towards certain races and nationalities.

4 _____ of the people in my country are prejudiced towards immigrants.

Us and them

In an experiment conducted in the United States during the height of the Vietnam War, researchers arranged for an actor to dress up as a protestor and attend a number of anti-war demonstrations. The actor's task was to pretend to become very ill during the protest, and request assistance to see how other protestors would react. Generally, the other protestors were very quick to assist the man to a first-aid station, and often even agreed to pay his bus fare so he could return home. Later, the researchers gave the actor a haircut, dressed him in conservative clothing, and handed him a pro-government sign to take to other anti-war demonstrations. When the actor pretended to be severely ill in these circumstances, the peace protestors were far less willing to come to his aid, despite his requests for help. Now, it seemed, he was no longer 'one of them'.

One unfortunate aspect of human character is the **tendency** to be biased against people who belong to different **racial**, religious, political and social groups. Researchers have found that people feel positive emotions such as admiration, sympathy and trust more easily for those categorized as being like them, and are quicker to feel negative emotions like suspicion and distrust when dealing with outsiders. Unfortunately, this bias has been documented in cultures all round the world, suggesting that this tendency might be hard-wired in the brain. In early human history, threats to our safety typically came from outsiders such as people from neighbouring tribes. Though this **instinct** may have served humanity well in the distant past, in modern society it can interfere with maintaining peace and international co-operation. Even in multi-cultural societies, such as those found in North America and Europe, people tend to naturally segregate themselves according to race, nationality, and other broad group categories. There are exceptions, of course, but for most people their friends tend to be very much like themselves.

This instinct to form groups and reject outsiders is the basis of stereotyping and prejudice. Stereotyping of those outside our group prevents us from seeing the individual. Once this occurs, it is easy to make assumptions that have a high probability of being false and grossly unfair. **Stereotypes** like 'people from country X are thieves', or 'people from country Y are selfish and rude', serve to put negative labels on outsiders, which can make discrimination seem justified. Once established, stereotypes are reinforced through confirmation bias; we see only the evidence which supports our assumptions. When we meet someone who does not fit a particular stereotype, we try to explain it away as an unusual exception or simply ignore it. People who hold negative beliefs about a particular group can be

45 surprised to find that, once they stop to think about it, very few of the people they actually know from that group come even close to matching the stereotypes.

There is also some evidence that an individual's self-esteem is a factor in promoting prejudice. One study manipulated the self-esteem of participants by randomly giving them very high or very low scores on an IQ test. Next, the researchers asked the
50 participants to evaluate two people in what the participants thought was an unrelated study. One of the people to be evaluated was of the same race as the participants, while the other was of a different race. Those whose self-esteem was boosted by the fake IQ test results gave both candidates similar scores, while those whose
55 self-esteem had been diminished gave much lower evaluation scores to the person from a different race. The researchers concluded that prejudice was used as a way of maintaining self-esteem. Indeed, subsequent research found that just getting people to engage in activities which improve their self-esteem results in a
60 reduction in negative views towards outside groups.

Saint Exupery once wrote, 'If I differ from you, far from wronging you, I enhance you.' Certainly there is nothing wrong with enjoying the company of people who belong to your own national, racial and social groups. However, people who limit themselves to
65 the familiar are in turn limited in how much they can learn and grow. Exposure to new ideas results from communicating with people who come from different backgrounds and have different perspectives on life. We have much to gain by overcoming the natural instinct to prefer our own kind, whilst distrusting those we know less well. In fact, the future of our species on this planet may
70 depend on it.

COMPREHENSION 1   **Decide if the sentences are True (T) or False (F). Then write the line number where the evidence is.**

1 In the first paragraph, the protestors tried to help anyone who was hurt or ill during the protests.

  T ☐   F ☐   Line number: _____

2 The article suggests that the tendency to distrust foreigners may be natural in humans.

  T ☐   F ☐   Line number: _____

3 People in countries which have many different races and cultures living together usually interact well with other races.

  T ☐   F ☐   Line number: _____

4 Stereotyping can make it easier to treat people badly.

T ☐   F ☐   Line number: _____

5 Most people form stereotypes based on evidence from personal experience.

T ☐   F ☐   Line number: _____

6 People with low IQs are more likely to be prejudiced against other races.

T ☐   F ☐   Line number: _____

7 People who feel good about themselves are less likely to be prejudiced against others.

T ☐   F ☐   Line number: _____

8 The article suggests that people benefit by interacting with others from different groups.

T ☐   F ☐   Line number: _____

COMPREHENSION 2   **Answer the questions without using a dictionary.**

1 In lines 1-2, what does *during the height of* mean?

  a the time of greatest activity
  b a high place
  c a time of great success

2 In line 12, what does *come to his aid* mean?

  a take him to a hospital or doctor
  b ask him for help
  c help him

3 In lines 21-22, what does *hard-wired in the brain* mean?

  a something that is learnt strongly from the environment
  b something that is naturally built into the brain
  c something that is too complex to understand

4 What statement best reflects lines 22-26?

  a Stereotyping has always been a problem for humans.
  b Long ago, distrust of foreigners may have been helpful to people, but now it can be harmful.
  c Distrust of foreigners is sometimes necessary, but at other times unnecessary.

5 In lines 26-29, what word means *to separate according to race, religion, sex*, etc.?

  _____

6 In line 35, what does *grossly* mean?

  a extremely

  b disgustingly

  c negatively

7 Which of the following would be a good example of the information given in lines 38-39?

  a Noticing that people of a certain race are more likely to commit crimes than other races.

  b Remembering all the times people of a certain country were rude, but forgetting all the times when people of that country were nice.

  c Believing that people of a certain race are dishonest, but then discovering that they are actually honest.

8 In line 47, what word means *to cause something to increase*?

  _____

9 Which statement best paraphrases the quote in lines 61-62?

  a If I am different from you, I help you to understand who you really are.

  b If I am different from you, I might hurt you in some ways, but I help you in other ways.

  c If I am different from you, I only make you better.

10 In line 65, what does the phrase *in turn* mean?

  a as a result

  b eventually

  c likely

SPEAKING **Discuss the questions with a partner.**

  1 Which parts of the reading do you agree with? What do you disagree with or question?

  2 What are some of the stereotypes of people from your country? In what ways do you match the stereotypes? In what ways are you different?

  3 How well do the people you know from other countries fit their national stereotypes?

VOCABULARY
FOCUS 1

Complete the sentences with the correct word.

courageous

inspiration

1   I think the referee has a _____ for the other team. He always makes calls in their favour.

    a assumption   **b** stereotype   **c** assist   **d** bias

2   I'm worried that all these action films will _____ the idea that violence is the best solution to all problems.

    a assume   **b** reinforce   **c** occur   **d** perceive

3   She said she was at work when the murder happened, but the police could not _____ her story.

    a perceive   **b** confirm   **c** aid   **d** identify

4   The _____ of winning a lot of money at a casino is quite low.

    a probability   **b** indication   **c** tendency   **d** barrier

5   You should not _____ that all people are basically good. There are some bad people out there.

    a ignore   **b** discriminate   **c** confirm   **d** assume

6   I felt that my last company _____ against women, as very few were promoted into managerial positions.

    a conducted   **b** discriminated   **c** established   **d** threatened

7   It wasn't easy succeeding on my own, but I was able to _____ all the difficulties.

    a overcome   **b** respond   **c** reject   **d** ignore

8   If you don't have any _____ that he stole the money, how can you fire him?

    a perspective   **b** evidence   **c** barrier   **d** exposure

VOCABULARY
FOCUS 2

Complete the sentences with the correct words. The words may need to be changed to match the sentence grammatically.

1   *discriminate/discrimination*

    a   The policy of our company is to prevent _____ based on race or nationality.

    b   We also do not _____ against gender.

2   *assist/assistance*

    a   I will be happy to _____ you to your room.

    b   If you need any further _____, do not hesitate to call the front desk.

3 *react/reaction*

    a She had a strong _____ to seeing Chris at the party.

    b If I had known she would _____ like that, I wouldn't have taken her to the party.

4 *threat/threaten*

    a Stephan got into trouble at school when he made a _____ on an internet site to hurt another student.

    b The head teacher _____ to have him kicked out of school permanently if it ever happened again.

5 *instinct/instinctively*

    a A young bird _____ knows when it is ready to fly.

    b Like all other _____, this skill is not taught to the bird.

Grammar Exemplification	We often introduce examples within a sentence using *like* and *such as*. *Even in multi-cultural societies, such as those found in North America and Europe…* *Stereotypes like 'people from country X are thieves'…*

GRAMMAR 1 **Complete the sentences with your own ideas.**

1 People from countries such as _____ often immigrate to my country.

2 There are some false stereotypes about people from my country like _____.

3 Films such as _____ reinforce negative stereotypes of some people.

4 Some entertainers in my country like _____ have become popular abroad.

5 I like musicians and music groups from foreign countries like _____.

GRAMMAR 2 **Write your own sentences. Give examples using *like* and *such as*.**

For example:

Kind of places you would like to travel to

I would like to visit places with beautiful natural scenery like New Zealand and South Africa.

1 Kind of places you would like to travel to

2 Kind of films you like the most

3 Kind of celebrities you find the most attractive

4 Kind of people that annoy you the most

5 Kind of teachers you like the most

6 Kind of food you like the most

Effective • *Skills*

Share your answers to the following questions with a partner.

1 In general, I …

  a am more attracted to people taller than I am.

  b am more attracted to people shorter than I am.

  c have no preference for height when considering who I go out with.

2 Can you sometimes judge people well just based on their appearance?

  a Often I can tell a lot about a person just by looking at their appearance

  b Sometimes I can judge appearances accurately, but at other times I am very wrong

  c I really don't trust myself to judge people by appearance only

3 What is your opinion regarding people who choose to have plastic surgery to make themselves more attractive?

  a Generally positive

  b Generally neutral

  c Generally negative

Judging books by their covers

Psychologists talk about the *physical attractiveness stereotype* to refer to our tendency to assume that attractive people also possess other desirable traits, such as happiness, success, kindness, and so on. Just like the stereotyping of other races and nationalities, these views can have very real and unfortunate outcomes.

The most common physical stereotype for men is height. The English language reflects this biased point of view. We '**look up to**' people we respect, yet '**look down on**' those who we have a low opinion of. Research has shown that people tend to rate tall men as more confident, masculine and capable than short men. What is perhaps even odder is that people's perceptions of height are often influenced by how they generally regard the person. In politics, for example, people who **favour** a certain male candidate generally

15 overestimate his height, and under-estimate the height of the opposing candidate. Tony Blair and William Hague, both 1.8 metres tall, were the leading candidates for the position of Prime Minister in the United Kingdom in 2001. A poll of voters' perceptions of their respective heights, however, found
20 that 64 per cent of voters thought Hague was short (less than 1.75 metres tall), whereas only 35 per cent of voters thought Blair was short. Perhaps it was no **coincidence** that Blair had a **landslide** election victory.

Facial appearance is important for most of us. The following
25 are common stereotypes in some western cultures:
- Good-looking men are considered more intelligent and able than less attractive men, yet for women the reverse can be perceived as true.
- Blonde girls are perceived as being less intelligent than **brunettes**.
30
- Men with beards are considered more masculine, but also less trustworthy.
- People with a 'baby face' (large eyes, small nose, small chin and a round face) are perceived as helpless,
35 dependent and affectionate.
- People with ugly faces are more likely to be judged **guilty** of a crime than people with attractive faces.

Now, here's the problem: there is no strong evidence that any of these perceptions are true. Height has no likely relationship
40 to intelligence or ability. The probability that men with beards are likely to be dishonest is no different than for men without. Some studies might suggest that certain physical features are related to personality traits and behaviours, but there is no clear evidence to support these claims. However, there does
45 seem to be evidence that when we view attractive people as more valuable members of society this does mean they are more likely to possess positive attributes such as self confidence, better social skills, jobs and incomes.

With such strong **unconscious** stereotypes of appearances,
50 who can blame people for wanting to get plastic surgery?

DISCUSSION

Considering the information in this reading, which of the following opinions do you agree with? Discuss with your partner.

1 Job interviews should be conducted by phone, not in person

2 Judges and juries should not be allowed to see the face of the person they are judging

3 Schools should do more to educate children about stereotypes

4 Government healthcare should include cosmetic plastic surgery

5 If the technology is available in the future, parents should have the right to select the height of their children

UNDERSTANDING VOCABULARY FROM CONTEXT

Match the words or expressions in bold in the text to the correct definitions (1-8).

1 a situation in which two things happen by chance at the same time _____

2 showing that you like or approve of something _____

3 a woman with dark, brown hair _____

4 a victory by a very large majority in an election _____

5 to think that you are better or more important than someone else _____

6 to admire or respect someone _____

7 a feeling or thought that you do not realize you have _____

8 to be found responsible for a crime _____

EXERCISE 1

Read the text.

Time out! The instant replay debate

In every sporting event, officials will **inevitably** make poor calls on the field which result in unfair outcomes. American football has <u>addressed</u> this issue by allowing coaches to challenge questionable calls by referees using instant replay technology. Many football fans were initially opposed to this intervention, but several years after its **implementation**, it has become an accepted part of the game. With the relative success of instant replays in American football, more and more people call for it to be used in other sporting events, particularly World Cup football. In games where the outcomes are too often determined solely by a single referee <u>call</u> (or non-call), to many it seems logical that this technology should be used to avoid the **tragedy** of blown calls. However, other fans argue that football and American football are different sports, and what <u>works</u> for one may well not work for the other. Football is a game that permits few <u>breaks</u>, and even occasional stops for instant replays may **disrupt** the flow of play.

EXERCISE 2

Complete the summary.

The text discusses the issue of whether or not sports should use (1)_____ technology. This has been successful in (2)_____, so a lot of people want to try it in (3)_____. It is argued that this can prevent bad (4)_____ from having an effect on the outcome of the game.

EXERCISE 3

Match the key words in **bold** from the text to the correct definitions (1–4).

1   Impossible to avoid or prevent.

    _____

2   A bad situation that makes people very upset or angry.

    _____

3   To prevent something from continuing.

    _____

4   Making something, such as an idea or plan, start to work and be used.

    _____

EXERCISE 4

The following words are <u>underlined</u> in the text. Choose the best definition.

1   *addressed*

    a   A formal speech

    b   To write a name and address on an envelope or package

    c   To try to deal with a problem or question

2   *call*

    a   A formal or public request that something should happen

    b   A decision that is the responsibility of a certain person

    c   The act of telephoning someone

3   *works*

    a   To succeed or have a particular effect

    b   To have a job

    c   To move something gradually

4   *breaks*

    a   Times in which one thing ends completely

    b   Opportunities that help you become successful

    c   Periods of time when you are not working and can rest

EXERCISE 1

Read the text and answer the questions in Exercise 2 as quickly as you can. Write your starting and finishing time.

Start time: _____

Finish time: _____

Teaching English abroad

People often wonder why native speakers of English go abroad to teach English. For some, language education is their chosen profession and they go abroad where the demand for native-speaker English teachers is strong. For many, though, teaching English abroad is a chance to travel and explore a new culture while making some money at the same time. Foreign teachers tend to stay just for a year or two, but most are sincere and work hard. As a matter of fact, quite a few end up pursuing language education as a career, and seek out training and education in teaching. Unfortunately, some people who go abroad to teach do not have a responsible attitude to their work and care little for the quality of their teaching. The excessive demand for native-speaker English teachers allows them to survive comfortably, despite their lack of qualifications and professionalism. It is this minority that gives other foreign teachers a bad name.

EXERCISE 2

Decide if the sentences are True (T), False (F), or if the information is Not Given (NG) in the text.

1   Native speakers of English have many opportunities to teach English abroad.

   T ☐   F ☐   NG ☐

2   Most native-English speakers who go abroad to teach English are qualified, professional teachers.

   T ☐   F ☐   NG ☐

3   Some people decide to become trained language teachers after they have tried teaching abroad for a year or two.

   T ☐   F ☐   NG ☐

4   It is difficult for unqualified and irresponsible foreign teachers to do well abroad.

   T ☐   F ☐   NG ☐

5   Low-quality English teaching by native speakers is very common in Europe.

   T ☐   F ☐   NG ☐

6   Most native-speaker English teachers have positive views of the countries in which they teach.

   T ☐   F ☐   NG ☐

EXERCISE 3

Complete the text with the words in the box. Use each word only once.

prejudiced	integrate	discrimination
minority	immigrants	stereotype

In almost every country in the world, (1)_____ races often suffer from (2)_____. Newly arrived (3)_____ to a country can have a particularly difficult experience in this regard. Although some races (4)_____ well into the new culture, others have difficulty adapting. People from the majority race can sometimes be (5)_____ against other races simply because people from these races look or act differently. This can result in the creation of a negative (6)_____ that gives the newcomers a bad image. In this age of globalization, people should make more effort to understand and respect people from different cultures.

11 Media

PRE-READING 1 **Complete the sentences with the key words in bold from the text.**

1 Governments should do more to protect _____ by punishing companies that make faulty or dangerous products.

2 One good thing about television _____ in some Asian countries is that they do not often interrupt a programme.

3 Many people _____ Japan with images of hard-working people and modern technology.

4 In an MBA programme, students learn the most recent _____ for successful management and leadership.

5 Pro golfer Michelle Wie reached _____ status even before she won any major competitions. She is more famous than even the top female golfers in the world!

6 Most people who buy music are teenagers, so recording companies produce bands that _____ to young people.

PRE-READING 2 **Discuss the questions with a partner.**

1 Think of some well-known television commercials. Do you think they are effective?

2 Which celebrities in your country appear most often in commercials and advertisements?

3 To what extent do you think you might be influenced by advertisements and television commercials to buy products?

    a sometimes strongly affected

    b only somewhat affected

    c not affected at all

Consumer beware: advertising techniques

Although most **commercials** only last 15–30 seconds, an astounding amount of time and money go into their production. Marketing agencies invest a lot of money into research in the most effective ways to persuade **consumers** to buy their products. Unfortunately, these methods typically rely on appeals to emotion rather than logic, and thus can effectively manipulate viewers into purchasing products that they really don't need. Media critics call for increased public awareness of advertising **techniques** and their potentially harmful effects.

1 The familiarity factor

The first goal of advertising is to make the public aware of and familiar with the product. For most people, brands are not chosen after researching the product and carefully comparing with competitors. Familiarity drives most of our decisions: we have heard the name before, and thus assume that it must be a safer choice than a product we have never heard about. In many cases, this sense of familiarity only comes from clever advertising campaigns, and not from more reliable sources.

2 Positive association

A fundamental advertising technique is to get viewers to make subconscious positive associations with their products. Images of love, family, people helping others, and so on are useful for this end. US media critic Bill Walsh notes, 'Many of the best commercials appeal to our feelings rather than to our reason. Hallmark cards, Kodak film, and McDonald's hamburgers realized long ago that if they could somehow associate themselves with wholesome values or good feelings, they'd increase sales.' The following are some of the common ways advertisers seek to associate their products with positive images.

- Symbols
  Advertisers make strategic use of powerful symbols to create positive associations with their products. Every society has its own symbols that stir patriotic, religious, or other kinds of strong emotions and advertisers often use these prominently in ads, even though there may be no logical connection between the symbol and the product. For example, the Statue of Liberty or the US flag are often shown in advertisements to evoke strong, positive feelings in North Americans.
  One technique common in a number of countries is the use of the English language in advertisements. A native English speaker might do a voice-over of the company slogan, or the ad might use famous

English language songs, for example. Even though the advertised product or service may have no connection with the English language, the United States, England, etc., the English language itself has become representative of prestige and upward mobility in many countries, and advertisers hope to make this association with their product.

- Celebrity endorsements
  Successful actors, singers, and athletes are employed not only to attract attention to the products, but also to make viewers **associate** the products with the successful image of the **celebrity**. We all know that the celebrities do not write the words they speak and they probably do not even use the product they endorse. Yet advertisers bank on consumers associating the product with the celebrities, and all the success and fame that go along with them.

3 Be a better person!

Commercials often **appeal** to our personal insecurities and desire to be loved and respected. 'Bandwagon' advertisements show many people enjoying the product together, while those who do not have the product are excluded from the group and thus are miserable. Other commercials link their products to images of people having fun and adventure (beer commercials being a particularly good example). Finally, many advertisements place their products in rich, luxurious backgrounds: even common items like washing machines and rice cookers. The underlying message? If you buy our products, you too can be like the people in the ads: accepted, happy, and respected.

4 But advertising doesn't affect me …

We all claim to be immune to advertising, but market research suggests that well-designed ad campaigns do have a strong effect on most people. True, whenever you see a commercial you might not immediately run out of your house to buy the product, but on some level it is very difficult not to be influenced. US advertising executive Stephen Garey notes that it is the cumulative effect of advertising that we need to be careful of the most. The combination of the tens of thousands of commercials we see day after day, year after year, drive the same message into our heads: to feel dissatisfied with our lives and ourselves unless we have the newest, latest, and best products.

This message is a lie. Love, happiness, friendships, popularity, and respect: none of these come from owning a product. Judging by rising levels of personal debt and a seemingly endless desire for more and more products, the effects of advertising on society are very real. Advertising will probably never go away, nor can we expect advertisers to change their tactics any time soon. However, being aware of the hidden messages in advertising can enable us to resist its seductive power.

COMPREHENSION 1   **Decide if the sentences are True (T) or False (F). Then write the line number where the evidence is.**

1   Commercials are most effective when they simply inform customers about the qualities of their products.

    T ☐   F ☐   Line number: _____

2   The text implies that most people make careful, well thought-out decisions when buying products.

    T ☐   F ☐   Line number: _____

3   If a commercial makes people think of things they love, they will be more likely to buy the advertised product.

    T ☐   F ☐   Line number: _____

4   Asian advertisers use the English language in their commercials to encourage people to learn English.

    T ☐   F ☐   Line number: _____

5   The text implies that advertisers usually want celebrities who use their products for their commercials.

    T ☐   F ☐   Line number: _____

6   The text suggests that people who think they are not affected by advertising are usually wrong.

    T ☐   F ☐   Line number: _____

7   The author implies that advertising causes people to spend more money than they have.

    T ☐   F ☐   Line number: _____

8   The text argues that companies must be forced to change the way they make advertisements.

    T ☐   F ☐   Line number: _____

COMPREHENSION 2   **Answer the questions without using a dictionary.**

1   In the first paragraph, which word means *to influence someone or control something in a dishonest way*? _____

2   In line 14, which word means *motivates*? _____

3   Which one of the following is implied from lines 14–18?

    a   Most of us do not really know about the products we use.

    b   Companies and corporations cannot be trusted.

    c   It is very difficult to get good information about products.

4 In line 22, what does the expression *for this end* refer to?

    a What eventually happens as a result of advertising.

    b For the purpose of making positive associations.

    c The way most commercials finish.

5 In line 30, which word means *carefully planned for a specific purpose*?

    _____

6 In line 40, what is a *voice-over*?

    a When someone lip syncs

    b The voice of someone who is not seen is used in the commercial

    c When someone makes a mistake on a recording and must do it again

7 Which statement is expressed in lines 43–45?

    The English language is used because …

    a it is a global language and advertisers want people from other countries to understand the commercials.

    b advertisers want to encourage viewers to improve their English.

    c it is associated with respect and moving to high levels of social class and success.

8 In line 53, *bank on* means …

    a predict.

    b save money.

    c depend on.

9 In line 64, what does *underlying* mean?

    a The true message that is not directly stated

    b The secondary message

    c The message that is not understood

10 In line 66, which word means *to not be affected*?

    _____

11 In lines 70-71, which phrase means *to some extent*?

    _____

12 Which of the following is the main point of lines 73–76?

    a Commercials have an increasingly negative effect on people over time.

    b Commercials have both positive and negative effects on viewers.

    c Products can serve an important role in helping people improve their lives.

SPEAKING **Discuss the questions with a partner.**

1 What is your general opinion onf the conclusions in the text?

   a Generally, the conclusions are accurate. Advertising has a very strong and negative effect on our society.

   b The conclusions are only partially accurate. Advertising does have an effect, but it might not be as bad as the text suggests.

   c The conclusions are mostly wrong. Few people are really affected negatively by advertising.

2 Do you know of any current commercials that use the techniques mentioned in the text?

VOCABULARY FOCUS 1 **Complete the text with the words in the box.**

brands	clever	displayed	endorses	slogan	led
characters	commercials	consumers	potential		

commercials *consumers*

clever?

Advertising is found in magazines and on TV (**1**)_____.
One particularly (**2**)_____ way companies target
(**3**)_____ is the use of product placements in popular
films. Their product is (**4**)_____ within the film in some
noticeable way. For example, in *I, Robot*, Will Smith's character
(**5**)_____ Converse shoes not only by wearing them, but
by referring to them several times. A Burger King sign along with its
(**6**)_____ ('It just tastes better') is clearly visible in *Men in
Black II*. Popular (**7**)_____ of watches such as Omega are
worn by the main (**8**)_____ in *Minority Report* and James
Bond films. Product placements have the (**9**)_____ to
be very successful. The most famous product placement is perhaps
the sweet Reese's Pieces in *E.T.*, which (**10**)_____ to an
increase of 65 per cent in sales.

VOCABULARY FOCUS 2 **Underline the word that does not belong in each group.**

For example:

nice	pleasant	<u>terrible</u>	fantastic
1 relate	deny	associate	link
2 involve	take in	admit	exclude
3 fundamental	basic	prominent	primary
4 permit	manipulate	control	influence
5 doubtful	reliable	questionable	suspicious
6 insecurity	confidence	esteem	assurance
7 expected	ordinary	typical	astounding
8 potential	possibility	restriction	capability

Grammar First and second conditionals	We use conditionals with *if*-clauses when we talk about the possibility of events. The first conditional indicates that we believe the event is possible or likely to happen. The present simple verb form is used in the *if*-clause, and the modals *can* or *will* are commonly used in the independent clause. *If you* **buy** *our products, you* **can be** *like the people in the ads.* *If you* **leave** *the party before 8pm, you* **will miss** *Rebecca.* The second conditional indicates that the speaker does not believe the event is possible or likely in the future; it is an imaginary, unreal situation. The past simple verb form is used in the *if*-clause and the modals *could* or *would* are used in the independent clause. *If a friend* **asked** *you to help her cheat in a test,* **would** *you* **do** *it?* *Even if you* **were** *a millionaire, I still* **wouldn't marry** *you.*

GRAMMAR 1 **Match the sentence halves to make logical statements.**

1 If I were the president,

2 If I become a politician,

3 If I had a lot of money,

4 If I earn a lot of money after I graduate,

5 If I do my homework well,

6 If I didn't spend so much time playing with my friends,

a I will move out of my parents' house immediately.

b I could really improve my marks.

c I would drive to school in a BMW.

d I would lower taxes.

e the final test will be a little easier.

f I will try to improve health care.

GRAMMAR 2 **Write conditional sentences with information about you. If the event is a real possibility, use the first conditional. If it is unlikely, use the second conditional.**

For example: get good grades this term

If I get good grades this term, I will be able to get a scholarship.

If I got good grades this term, my mother would be shocked.

1 get good grades this semester

2 get a job in a big company

3 become rich and famous

4 marry someone from another country

5 get married before the age of 27

6 travel somewhere next year

Effective • *Skills*

DISCUSSION **How often do you feel it is necessary to replace or upgrade the following possessions?**

Computer

Mobile phone

Your wardrobe

Your car

PREDICTING **Look at the title and read the first sentence of each paragraph. What do you expect the text to be about?**

a The dangers of spending too much money

b How some people managed to live without unnecessary shopping

c How to shop for new things without spending too much money

d How careful shopping is important to the growth of a country's economy.

The simple life

In this age of consumerism, many people are finding themselves overloaded with possessions and with a seemingly irrational desire for even more, probably as a result of the countless advertisements we are exposed to year after year. How many possessions do we really need to
5 be happy? How often do we actually need to update our mobile phones, computers, and wardrobe? With advertisers finding new ways to get people to buy their products, a movement towards living a simpler non-consumer life is taking root.

US newspaper columnist Craig Wilson spent all of 2003 spending the
10 least amount of money possible. He allowed himself to purchase books and music (necessary, he says, for their nurturing value) and gifts for friends and family. Otherwise, he would not permit himself to buy anything new. Although he had to make a point of avoiding certain stores (too much temptation), he was able to achieve his goal. He
15 claims the experience was cleansing, and he continues to keep shopping to a minimum. Popular author Judith Levine followed with a book entitled *Not Buying It, My Year without Shopping*. Levine came up with the idea

after a holiday season in which she, once again, maxed out her credit cards. She too found the experiment worthwhile. The word got out.

20 In 2006, a group of ten friends in San Francisco took the idea on to the community level and made a pledge to live as cheaply as possible for a year. They called this pledge the *compact*, after the Mayflower Compact, a social contract created by the first Pilgrims to North America whose purpose was to build a city on a hill that would be a model for the whole

25 world to see. The San Francisco friends posted their agreement online and attracted thousands of supporters, many of whom promised to join as well. An appearance on US TV led to global publicity and more members joined the compact from around the world. Said one of the founding members, John Perry, 'We set out to do this as a challenge

30 among ourselves. We never intended to start a movement or dictate what people should or shouldn't do, so we're pleased to have so many others talking about our consumerist culture.'

The compact followed two rules: 1) Don't buy new products of any kind (from stores, websites, etc.), and 2), either borrow or buy used

35 merchandise. They allowed several exceptions to the rules:

- Food, drink, and necessary medicine
- Necessary cleaning products (but not cleaning equipment)
- Socks and underwear
- Utilitarian services (plumbers, electricians, car mechanics, vets,

40   etc.)
- Charitable contributions
- Magazines, newspapers (renewals only, no new subscriptions). If possible, do more reading online
- DVD rentals and downloadable music files (freely shared and legal,

45   please)

Although a few members failed to follow the rules at times, the group generally succeeded and most of them continue their pledge to this day. Says Rachel, 'The real revelation is that it isn't that hard. We all have so much stuff, we could probably live for years without replacing anything. It

50 makes you change the way you look at things and appreciate what you have.' She estimates that she saved $4,000 that year.

There are critics of the simplicity movement, however. Author Ted Nordhaus warns that the simplicity movement is unlikely to be successful on a large scale. Developing nations, where the bulk of

55 factories are located and millions of labourers find much needed employment, need markets for what they produce. 'We can't sacrifice

our way out of this problem,' he says. 'To live is to consume, and only technology and innovation can begin to address these global issues.'

60 Though living more simply may not solve all of the world's problems, many of us could reconsider our consumption practices that are putting a strain on our natural resources and add to rising levels of pollution. Indeed, in times when money is short worldwide, more people will be reducing their spending out of necessity, rather than out of concern for the environment. Regardless of the motivation, radically
65 rethinking the ways we spend money and value possessions may be just what the world needs.

SUMMARY COMPLETION

Complete the summary with the words in the box.

possessions	critics	simplify	reduce	consumerism
permit	attracted	experiment	exceptions	movement

Due to the perceived negative effects of _____, many people are making an effort to _____ their amount of spending. They try to _____ their lives by shopping less for new products they may not really need. A few years ago, several noted authors tried an _____ in which they did not _____ themselves to buy anything new which was not a necessity for a year. They wrote positively about the results.

A group of friends in San Francisco then _____ a lot of publicity with their plan to avoid buying new products. They did allow for some _____ to their no-shopping rules, such as food and medicine. There are some _____ of this trend, however, who do not believe the simplicity _____ will be largely successful. But many people still think it is necessary to reconsider the value we place on obtaining new _____.

DISCUSSION

Discuss with a partner.

1 Which of the following opinions in the reading most closely matches your own?

   a The future of our planet depends on more people consuming less

   b The basic idea of consuming less is good, but the groups in the reading take it too far

   c The idea that more people should consume less is impractical and unnecessary

2 In your case, what would be the most difficult aspect of spending a year without buying anything new?

12 · Success

PRE-READING 1 **Complete the sentences with the key words in bold from the text.**

1 Company _____ are always looking for intelligent and motivated graduates from top universities.

2 Once hired by a company, new _____ can expect to go through a training programme.

3 In most cases, job _____ are required to first submit CVs and then wait to be contacted by the company for an interview.

4 During the job interview, some interviewers try to ask very difficult questions to see how the _____ will react under pressure.

PRE-READING 2 **Tick (✔) the suggestions you think are good advice for a job interview. Compare your answers with a partner.**

1 ☐ Avoid using gestures while you speak.

2 ☐ Speak confidently, but not too proudly.

3 ☐ Speak quickly and clearly.

4 ☐ Learn good answers to common interview questions from websites on the Internet.

5 ☐ Worry more about *how* you say your answers than *what* you say.

6 ☐ Be careful with your behaviour even before you go into the interview room.

For an effective interview

A director in the human resources department of a large international company advises job applicants at interview stage in the employment process.

How should the job applicant dress?

Be ready to invest in your interview clothes, since this reflects your determination to join the company. Also, neat clothing with attention to detail usually reflects an organized and careful character, so make sure your tie is straight and your shoes are polished, for those little details can be determining factors in the outcome of your interview. Most important of all, pick an outfit that suits you well and gives you confidence.

How should the job applicant speak?

It is most important to be confident, but modest. This is a difficult balance that can only be acquired through years of practice in everyday life. Mention your strengths and accomplishments, but do so in a 'matter of fact' tone that does not come across as arrogant. Make it clear that even though you have many good qualities, you realize you still need to learn more and improve.

Moderate use of gestures is effective. They grasp the interviewer's attention as well as make you more persuasive. However, continuous and exaggerated hand movements can have a negative effect. Also, unnecessary body movements such as nervously bouncing your leg can reveal a lack of confidence. Smile throughout the interview, but be careful not to look indifferent or condescending. Don't speak too fast. It is natural to speak faster when under pressure, so try to speak slower than usual at an interview. Humour can be helpful in lightening the atmosphere of the interview, but there is the risk of the interview losing focus, so be careful.

In the interview, what qualities are you looking for?

An interview's main purpose is not to determine who is nicer, smarter, or more hard-working. It is a process to find a person who will most suit the company, and give one hundred per cent. Through the interview, a company tries to judge whether the applicant has the qualities the company needs, and has seriously considered and understood what having a job means.

- **Quality**

  For potential **recruits** just out of university, **applicants** are not expected to have many job skills and even if they do, the job skills

40   acquired during university life are not the same as those needed in
      the actual workplace. Academic excellence and a positive attitude
      towards learning are what many **recruiters** look for. Academic
      achievement shows the applicant has curiosity and the mental
      capacity to satisfy that curiosity.

      • **Attitude**

45   In the workplace, you may be called upon to sacrifice your personal
      time as you are now part of a team and must act according to the
      needs of the company. Companies look for future employees who
      pursue their career with passion and have a sense of professional-
      ism. This is why the recruiter looks for someone who will adjust
50   well to the working environment and not just for someone with
      outstanding accomplishments.

      **What kind of answers to common interview questions
      are not effective?**
      The Internet has allowed the sharing of answers to interview
55   questions and 'model' self-introductions are also circulating on the
      Internet. Recruitment teams in companies are aware of this and are
      monitoring the main online communities. 'Model' interview answers
      from these communities are easily caught, and have a negative impact
      on the applicant's interview result, as this shows a lack of creativity as
60   well as honesty.

      What kinds of answers are likely to impress you?
      Personally, as the director of human resources, I pay more attention to
      the body language of the **interviewee**, not to the answers. The
      interviewee cannot give his or her best answers under so much
65   pressure, and focusing too much on spoken details will interfere with
      the evaluation of his or her character. Thus, I am more impressed by
      posture, eye contact, and *how* an interviewee answers a question.

      That being said, there are certainly answers which can make a very
      bad impression. Do your research on the company and the position
70   you are applying for before the interview so you can be prepared to
      answer questions well.

      **What kind of English language skills do you look for in
      interviews?**
      Companies use various methods to evaluate English proficiency.
75   Students should study business English and develop their English
      speaking skills not just to get into a company, but also to do well after
      they get in. Advanced English ability is not always mandatory for
      company positions, but generally people find that those with an
      excellent command of English have better career opportunities than
80   those who struggle with the language.

COMPREHENSION 1 **Decide if the sentences are True (T) or False (F). Then write the line number where the evidence is.**

1 Small details in how you dress can make a big difference in the interview.

T ☐   F ☐   Line number: _____

2 When hiring new recruits, companies don't always look for people who already have a lot of work experience.

T ☐   F ☐   Line number: _____

3 Having the right attitude can be even more important than having an impressive CV.

T ☐   F ☐   Line number: _____

4 When answering questions, speaking quickly does not make a good impression.

T ☐   F ☐   Line number: _____

5 The Internet should be used to get information on how to answer questions and for model self-introductions.

T ☐   F ☐   Line number: _____

6 Getting good marks at school is an indication that you might be able to learn well in a company.

T ☐   F ☐   Line number: _____

7 If you work hard and sacrifice your free time for the company, you have an excellent chance of becoming a CEO.

T ☐   F ☐   Line number: _____

8 English skills are only important for getting into a company.

T ☐   F ☐   Line number: _____

COMPREHENSION 2 **Answer the questions without using a dictionary.**

1 In line 6, what is the meaning of *attention to detail*?

a wearing a suit and tie
b dressing carefully
c choosing designer clothes

2 In line 9, what does the word *suits* mean?

a a set of formal clothing
b matches, meets the needs of something
c look attractive

3 Reread lines 45-49. Which of the following statements are true?

   a Company life demands many sacrifices, but gives you the chance of having great rewards later.

   b Company life is very difficult for three years, but then conditions improve greatly.

   c Company life is very difficult, but all who work hard will eventually become leaders in the company.

   d Company life is difficult and very few succeed, so plan on quitting after three years or so.

4 Which word in lines 54-56 means *go from person to person*?

   _____

5 In line 62, which word indicates that this advice may just be this particular person's own view? _____

6 Which statement best summarizes lines 77-80?

   a Good English skills are needed to get a job and to keep the position

   b There are very few careers in the business world which do not require regular use of the English language

   c Not all employees need to use English, but strong English skills make it easier to advance to higher positions

SPEAKING   **Discuss the questions with a partner.**

1 Which advice in the text did you find most interesting or useful?

2 Have you ever had an interview for any kind of position or job? How did it go? Did you make any of the mistakes noted in the text?

VOCABULARY   **Complete the sentences with the words in the box. Then ask**
FOCUS 1   **and answer the questions with a partner**

confidence   outstanding   impact   balance
invest   modest   monitor   moderate

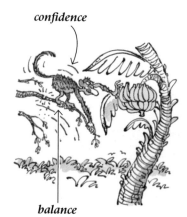

confidence

balance

1 Do you prefer a boyfriend or girlfriend who is quite _____? Or is it OK if he/she is a bit proud?

2 Do you consider yourself a light, _____, or heavy drinker?

3 Do you maintain a good _____ between studying hard and relaxing? Or do you do either one too much?

4 In what school subject do you consider yourself _____ (or at least slightly above average)?

impact

5 Some employers _____ emails sent out by their employees. Do you think it is OK for employers to check up on their employees like this?

6 Do you have _____ that you will get a good job after graduation? Or are you unsure?

7 Do you think the way you dress at a job interview can have a big _____? Or do you think it is not very important?

8 In future, do you think you will _____ much money in businesses? Or do you think that it is too risky?

VOCABULARY FOCUS 2

Complete the sentences with the correct word.

1 *curious/curiosity*

   a Cindy is very _____ about new cultures.

   b To satisfy her _____, she travels as much as she can.

2 *confident/confidence*

   a _____ can make almost any person look attractive.

   b A person who isn't _____ at all, however, is usually less attractive, regardless of what he or she looks like.

3 *humorous/humour*

   a Many women like men who have a good sense of _____.

   b For some reason, however, men are not always attracted to _____ women.

4 *passionate/passion*

   a Fuji is quite _____ about his future career: accounting.

   b His friends can't understand how he can have a _____ for something like that.

5 *modest/modesty*

   a _____ is a quality that is valued slightly more in the East than in the West.

   b However, people in the West still like others who are more _____ than proud.

6 *persuasive/persuasiveness*

   a Being able to make a _____ speech is an extremely important skill for future business persons.

   b In job interviews, recruiters often look for evidence that interviewees have potential for _____.

Grammar	When giving advice or opinions, we often use the following structure:
It is + adjective + infinitive	*It is* + adjective + infinitive **It is important to sleep** well the night before an interview. **It is natural to be** nervous during a test or interview. **It is not easy to have** an interview in a second language.

GRAMMAR 1   **Rewrite the sentences using the *It is* structure.**

For example:

Being prepared for interviews is very important.

It is very important to be prepared for interviews.

1   Being early for a job interview is good.

2   Dressing formally is crucial for a successful interview.

3   Asking questions is not so important in job interviews in Asia.

4   Asking the interviewer how much money he/she earns is rude.

5   Putting your feet up on the interviewer's desk during an interview is unacceptable.

6   Making good eye contact during the interview is quite important.

GRAMMAR 2   **Write advice for preparing for tests. Discuss your sentences with a partner.**

1   The night before the test, it is important to _____.

2   When taking a test, it is not easy to _____.

3   During a class, it is good to _____.

4   When reading in English, it is _____ to _____.

GRAMMAR 3   **Write *It is … to …* sentences for the topics using the words in the box.**

good	not good	impossible	possible
easy	not easy	important	not necessary

1   make notes

2   stay awake

3   get an A grade

4   get to a class on time

5   copy from other students

6   use an English-English dictionary

Effective • *Skills*

What does being successful mean to you? Use the following prompts to help you.

1 Being successful in my career means having _____.

2 If I can _____, then I will consider my life a success.

3 For me, my life will be a success if I can _____.

Ingredients of success

Put your heart, mind, intellect, and soul into even your smallest acts. This is the secret of success. Swami Sivanandi

In 2002, researchers Taylor and Humphrey analyzed interviews made with 80 UK and US business leaders, drawn from a wide range of businesses. They identified the skills and attributes which were most common among those who had been successful at Chief Executive level. Although most (91 per cent) had a university degree and
5 relevant technical skills, success was not closely linked to a level or type of knowledge: few had business degrees or outstanding technical ability.

Characteristics of successful chief executives
The chief executive officers (CEOs) worked very long hours—but loved their work. They enjoyed leadership and recognition. They were noticeably self-
10 confident and good at communicating with others, and putting interviewers at their ease. Their excellent interpersonal skills included patience and tolerance, often learnt through the job itself. They were energetic, but took care to manage stress levels and stay healthy. Male directors were more sensitive to variations in their emotional lives and needed emotional stability in order to succeed. Most had
15 a wide range of interests and part of what they brought to a company was '**breadth** of vision developed from a wide range of experience.' Most of these are self-management and people skills rather than unusual abilities or technical skills.

Attributes associated with success
The surprising outcome of Taylor and Humphrey's survey was that the range of
20 personal skills and qualities associated with success were ones that most people could **nurture**. The researchers wrote: 'Board directors are not a **race apart** ... we found ourselves in the presence of bright, hard-working people, but not creatures from another planet. They had a variety of IQs, expertise, and backgrounds. In other words, directors are just like the rest of us—and their positions are **up for**
25 **grabs**.' The skills and attitudes of successful people can be developed by others.

The main skills valued by the CEOs included:

- self-knowledge and self-awareness—this was especially noticeable, and the directors were frank about their skills and their **shortcomings**.
- interpersonal skills, especially the ability to work with, and lead, teams.
- problem-solving ability, using creative approaches and positive attitudes.
- a desire to win, especially on behalf of the company or team.
- a willingness to work very long hours and to '**do what it takes**'.
- emotional intelligence, especially when relating to others.
- the ability to manage stress and to take care of their health.
- a love of change.
- confidence.
- a broad range of personal interests.
- readiness to seize opportunities rather than making **rigid** personal plans.

Many of these skills have long been recognized as essential in the caring professions. It may be surprising to find this list associated with business success. However, similar skills are likely to be required across a very wide range of professions. Increasingly, employers expect employees to be able to work on project teams on complex problems. This requires many of the other skills listed: good people skills, emotional intelligence, self-knowledge, a positive attitude, a willingness to put the team's interests first. Negative thinking, selfish people who lack confidence, who get easily stressed, fear change, or who are not aware of how they are coping with their own emotions, are unlikely to be a great **asset** to a team.

However, the qualities needed for different kinds of success may vary from the above list. Academic success requires a willingness to refine analytical thinking skills. Successful relationships may require a willingness not to work very long hours outside of the home, but are still likely to require a willingness to 'do what it takes' to achieve a successful outcome for the relationship. High levels of success in any field tend to require long hours, hard work, practice, and a willingness to keep going towards achieving the goal even when you do not feel like it, or when you are tired or want to give up. There are few areas of life where an individual is unlikely to benefit from the characteristics associated with chief executives.

From the book *Skills for Success* by Stella Cottrell (2003)

COMPREHENSION   ## Tick (✔) all the qualities mentioned in the text.

1 ☐ Following orders well

2 ☐ Being able to look busy, even if you are not

3 ☐ Being willing to work overtime

4 ☐ Being able to work well with other people

5 ☐ Understanding your own strengths and weaknesses

6 ☐ Knowing how to get people to do what you want

7 ☐   Being consistent and firm

8 ☐   Being capable of focusing all your energy and attention on the company

9 ☐   Finding new ways to solve problems

10 ☐   Knowing how to speak respectfully to those in higher positions

UNDERSTANDING VOCABULARY FROM CONTEXT

Match the words or expressions in bold in the text to the correct definitions (1–8).

1   do anything necessary to succeed   _____

2   a wide range of different things   _____

3   not easily changed   _____

4   a major benefit   _____

5   be fundamentally different from others   _____

6   grow and develop   _____

7   weakness   _____

8   be available for other people to try to get   _____

DISCUSSION

Complete the table and discuss your answers with a partner. Which skills do you wish to improve? How can you improve them?

Skill	Good	Wish to improve	Not relevant to me
Self-knowledge and self-awareness			
Problem-solving ability			
A creative approach			
Positive attitude			
People skills			
Team-working			
Leadership			
A desire to succeed			
A willingness to do what it takes			
Emotional intelligence			
Ability to manage stress			
The ability to cope with and promote change			
Self-confidence			
A broad range of personal interests			
Self-knowledge			
Ability to cope with uncertainty			

[*Skills for Success* Stella Cottrell (2003)]

EXERCISE 1

Read the text.

Your attention, please

Any parent can tell you that infants find TV commercials more interesting to watch than programmes. The reason? Commercials effectively grab children's attention by providing a rapid series of images that make the visual experience unusual. When producing commercials for TV, the content of the commercial is secondary to this well-crafted **array** of imagery. Each image lasts for at most a few seconds before being replaced by another exciting image to **ensure** our attention does not **wander**. This filming technique may well have significant **adverse** effects on viewers, especially children. Researchers have found that young children who watch TV often are more likely to develop low attention **spans** that can **hinder** learning later in life. Commercials may be one of the primary reasons why this happens.

EXERCISE 2

Correct the sentences about the text.

1 The text discusses the advantages and disadvantages of watching TV commercials.

2 Companies are primarily concerned with informing consumers about their product.

3 Commercials are filmed in such a way that they are difficult to pay attention to.

4 Negative effects of television commercials on children are often only temporary.

EXERCISE 3

Match the key words in **bold** from the text to the correct definitions (1–6).

1 To make certain something happens or is done

_____

2 The amount of time that something lasts

_____

3 To stop something from making progress

_____

4 A large group of things that are related in some way

_____

5 To stop concentrating and start thinking about other things

_____

6 Not good or likely to cause problems

_____

EXERCISE 1

Read the text and answer the questions in Exercise 2 as quickly as you can. Write your starting and finishing time.

Start time: _____

Finish time: _____

Interview don'ts

A recent survey of human resource directors in the UK uncovered some common mistakes that job applicants make in the interview process. Chief among the complaints was a lack of preparation for the process. Many applicants neglect to do basic research on the company they are applying to and are thus unable to tell interviewers why they want to work in their company, and how they can be of benefit to it. Some applicants make spelling mistakes on their CVs and generally exhibit poor writing skills, and others fail to follow the application process correctly and fail to submit all the necessary documents. These errors reveal a lack of direction, responsibility and initiative that will probably carry over into the professional duties of the position. If you fail to prepare properly during the application process, what guarantee do employers have that you will handle your work responsibilities professionally?

EXERCISE 2

Decide if the sentences are True (T), False (F), or if the information is Not Given (NG) in the text.

1   The text lists typical reasons why job seekers fail.

T ☐   F ☐   NG ☐

2   Most mistakes mentioned in the text happen during the job interview.

T ☐   F ☐   NG ☐

3   Even small mistakes can result in failure to get the job.

T ☐   F ☐   NG ☐

4   Most people fail to prepare well for the interview process because they do not have enough time.

T ☐   F ☐   NG ☐

5   One common mistake is not properly reading all the necessary documents before the interview.

T ☐   F ☐   NG ☐

6   Companies believe that applicants who make small mistakes during the application and interview process will not be responsible workers.

T ☐   F ☐   NG ☐

Effective *Vocabulary*

The following are words from this book which are very common in academic settings.

Base word	Common forms	Translation/model sentence
academy	academia, *academic*, academically	
access	accessibility, accessible, inaccessible, accessed, accessing	
accurate	accuracy, accurately, inaccuracy, inaccurate	
achieve	achievable, achievement, achieved, achieving	
acknowledge	acknowledgment, acknowledged, acknowledging	
acquire	*acquisition*, acquired, acquiring	
adapt	adaptability, adaptable, *adaptation*, adaptive, adapted, adapting	
administer	*administration*, administrative, administratively, administrator	
affect	affective, affectively, affected, affecting, unaffected	
alternative	alternatively	
analyze	*analysis*, analyst, analysts, analytic, analytical, analytically, analyzed, analyzing	
annual	annually	
appreciate	appreciable, appreciably, appreciated, appreciating, *appreciation*, unappreciated	
approach	approachable, unapproachable, approached, approaching	
appropriate	appropriately, appropriateness, inappropriate, inappropriately	
area		
aspect	*aspects*	
assign	*assigned*, assigning, assignment, reassign, unassigned	

Base word	Common forms	Translation/model sentence
assist	*assistance*, assistant, assisted, assisting, unassisted	
assume	assumed, assuming, assumption	
attain	attainable, *attained*, attaining, attainment, unattainable	
attitude	*attitudes*	
attribute	attributable, *attributed*, attributing, attributes, attribution	
author	authored, authoring, authorship	
automate	automatic, automated, automating, *automatically*, automation	
available	availability, unavailable	
aware	awareness, unaware	
behalf	on behalf of ~	
benefit	beneficial, beneficiary, benefits, benefited, benefiting	
capable	capabilities, capability, incapable	
capacity		
category	*categories*, categorization	
chapter		
circumstance		
commit	*commitment*, committed, committing	
community	communities	
complex	complexities, complexity	
component		
compound	compounded, compounding	
compute	computation, computational, computable, *computer*, computed, computerized, computing	
conclude	concluded, concluding, *conclusion*, conclusive, conclusively, inconclusive, inconclusively	
conduct	conducted, conducting	
confirm	confirmation, *confirmed*, confirming	
conflict	conflicted, conflicting	

Base word	Common forms	Translation/model sentence
conform	conformed, conforming, conformist, *conformity*, nonconformist, nonconformity	
consequent	consequence, consequently	
considerable	considerably	
consist	consisted, consisting, consistency, *consistent*, consistently, inconsistencies, inconsistency, inconsistent	
constant	constancy, constantly	
consume	*consumer*, consumption	
context	contextual, contextualize, contextualized, contextualizing, uncontextualized	
contract	contracted, contracting, contractor	
contradict	*contradiction*, contradictory	
contrary	contrarily	
contrast	contrastive, contrasted, contrasting	
convene	*convention*, convened, convening, conventionally, unconventional	
convince	*convinced*, convincing, convincingly, unconvinced	
corporate	corporation	
correspond	corresponded, correspondence, corresponding, correspondingly	
create	created, creating, creation, creative, creatively, creativity, creator, recreate	
credit	credited, crediting, creditor	
culture	*cultural*, culturally, cultured, uncultured	
data		
debate	debated, debating, debatable	
decade	*decades*	
decline	declined, declining	
define	definable, defined, defining, *definition*, redefine, redefined, redefining, undefined	

Base word	Common forms	Translation/model sentence
definite	definitely, definitive, indefinite, indefinitely	
demonstrate	demonstrated, demonstrating, demonstrable, demonstrably, demonstration, demonstrative, demonstratively, demonstrator	
deny	denied, denying, deniable, denial, undeniable	
depress	depressed, depressing, *depression*	
design	designed, designer, designing	
despite		
diminish	*diminished*, diminishing, diminution, undiminished	
discriminate	*discriminated, discriminating, discrimination*	
distinct	*distinction*, distinctive, distinctively, distinctly, indistinct, indistinctly	
distort	*distorted*, distorting, distortion	
distribute	distributed, distributing, *distribution*, distributional, distributive, distributor, redistribute, redistributed, redistributing, redistribution	
domestic	domestically, domesticate, domesticated	
dominate	dominance, *dominant*, dominated, dominating, domination	
drama	*dramatic*, dramatically, dramatist, dramatization, dramatize	
economy	*economic*, economical, economically, economics, economist, uneconomical	
eliminate	eliminated, eliminating, elimination	
emphasis	emphasize, emphasized, emphasizing, emphatic, emphatically	
enhance	*enhanced*, enhancing, enhancement	
ensure	ensured, ensuring	
environment	environmental, environmentalist, environmentally	
establish	*established*, establishment	
estimate	estimated, estimating, estimation, overestimate, underestimate	

Base word	Common forms	Translation/model sentence
ethnic	ethnicity	
evaluate	evaluated, evaluating, *evaluation*, re-evaluate	
evident	*evidence*, evidential, evidently	
evolve	evolved, evolving, *evolution*, evolutionary, evolutionist	
exceed	exceeded, exceeding	
exclude	*excluded*, excluding, exclusion, exclusionary, exclusive, exclusively	
expert	expertise, expertly	
expose	exposed, exposing, *exposure*	
facilitate	facilitated, facilitating, facilitation, facility	
factor	factored, factoring, *factors*	
feature	featured, featuring	
final	finalize, finalized, finalizing, finality, finally, finals	
flexible	*flexibility*, inflexible, inflexibility	
focus	focused, focusing, refocus	
foundation	foundations	
function	functional, functionally, functioned, functioning	
fundamental	fundamentally	
furthermore		
generation		
globe	*global*, globally, globalization	
guarantee	guaranteed, guaranteeing	
guideline	*guidelines*	
identify	identifiable, identification, *identified*, *identifying*, identity, unidentifiable	
ignorant	ignorance, ignore, *ignored*, ignoring	
image	imagery	
immigrate	immigrated, immigrating, immigrant, *immigration*	

Base word	Common forms	Translation/model sentence
impact	impacted, impacting	
imply	implied, implying, *implication*	
impose	*imposed*, imposition	
income		
indicate	indicated, indicating, indication, indicative, indicator	
individual	individuality, individualism, individualist, individualistic, individually	
inevitable	inevitability, *inevitably*	
initial	initially	
injure	injured, injuring, *injury*, uninjured	
innovate	*innovation*, innovative, innovator	
institute	institution	
integrate	integrated, integrating, *integration*	
intense	intensely, intensify, *intensity*, intensive, intensively	
interact	interacted, interacting, *interaction*, interactive, interactively	
intermediate		
invest	*invested, investing, investment*, investor, reinvestment, reinvests	
investigate	investigated, investigating, *investigation*, investigative, investigator	
involve	*involved*, involvement, involving, uninvolved	
issue	issued, issuing	
item	itemization, itemize, itemized, itemizing	
journal		
justify	justifiable, justifiably, *justification*, justified, justifying, unjustified	
labour	laboured, labouring	
lecture	lectured, lecturing, lecturer	
legal	legality, legally, illegal, illegality, illegally	
link	linkage, linked, linking	
locate	located, locating, location, relocate	

Base word	Common forms	Translation/model sentence
logic	illogical, illogically, logical, logically	
maintain	maintained, maintaining, maintenance	
major	majority	
manipulate	manipulated, manipulating, *manipulation*, manipulative	
maximize	max, maximization, maximized, maximizing, *maximum*	
mental	mentality, mentally	
method	methodical, methodological, methodology	
minimum	minimal	
minor	minor, minorities, minority, minors	
monitor	monitored, monitoring, unmonitored	
motive	motivated, motivating, motivation, unmotivated	
negate	negative, negatively, negatives	
nonetheless		
normal	abnormal, abnormally, normalization, normalize, normalized, normalizing, normality, normally	
notion		
obtain	obtainable, *obtained*, obtaining, unobtainable	
occur	occurred, occurrence, occurring, reoccur	
odd	oddity	
ongoing		
option	optional	
outcome		
overall		
participate	participant, participated, participating, *participation*, participatory	
perceive	perceived, perceiving, perception	
per cent	percentage	
period	periodic, periodical, periodically	

Base word	Common forms	Translation/model sentence
phenomenon	phenomena, phenomenal	
philosophy	philosopher, philosophical, philosophically, philosophize, philosophized, philosophizing	
physical	physically	
policy		
positive	positively	
potential	potentially	
predict	predictability, predictable, predictably, predicted, predicting, prediction, unpredictability, unpredictable	
previous	previously	
primary	primarily	
principle	principled, unprincipled	
process	processed, processing, procession	
promote	promoted, promoting, promoter, promotions	
proportion	proportional, proportionally, proportionate, proportionately, disproportionately	
psychology	psychological, psychologically, psychologist	
publish	*published*, publishing, publisher, unpublished	
purchase	purchased, purchasing, purchaser	
pursue	pursued, pursuing, pursuit	
radical	radically, radical (n)	
range	ranged, ranging	
ratio		
react	reacted, reacting, reaction, reactionary, reactive, reactivate, reactor	
refine	refined, refining, refinement	
region	regional, regionally	
reinforce	reinforced, reinforcing, reinforcement	
reject	*rejected*, rejecting, rejection	

Base word	Common forms	Translation/model sentence
relevant	relevance, irrelevance, irrelevant	
reluctance	*reluctant*, reluctantly	
rely	reliability, reliable, reliably, *reliance*, reliant, relied, relying, unreliable	
remove	removable, removal, removed, removing	
require	required, requiring, requirement	
research	researched, researching, researcher	
resource	resourceful, unresourceful	
respond	responded, responding, respondent, *response*, responsive, responsiveness, unresponsive	
restrict	*restricted*, restricting, restriction, restrictive, restrictively, unrestricted, unrestrictive	
reveal	revealed, revealing, revelation	
reverse	reversal, reversed, reversing, reversible, irreversible	
rigid	rigidity, rigidly	
role		
secure	insecure, insecurity, secured, securely, securing, *security*	
seek	*sought*	
select	selected, selecting, selection, selective, selectively, selector	
series		
sex	sexism, sexual, sexually, sexuality	
significant	significance, significantly, signify, insignificant, insignificantly	
similar	similarity, similarly, dissimilar	
site		
source	sourced, sourcing	
specify	specifiable, specified, specifying, unspecified	
stable	stabilization, stabilize, *stability*, instability, unstable	
status		

Base word	Common forms	Translation/model sentence
straightforward		
strategy	strategic, strategically, strategist	
structure	structural, structurally, structured, structuring, restructure, restructured, restructuring, unstructured	
submit	submission, submitted, submitting	
sufficient	sufficiency, insufficient, insufficiently, sufficiently	
survey	surveyed, surveying	
sustain	*sustainable*, sustainability, sustained, sustaining, sustenance, unsustainable	
symbol	*symbolic*, symbolically, symbolize, symbolized, symbolizing, symbolism	
target	targeted, targeting	
task		
technical	technically	
technique		
technology	technological, technologically	
temporary	temporarily	
tense	*tension*, tensely, tensions	
text	textual	
theory	theoretical, theoretically, theorist	
tradition	*traditional*, traditionalist, traditionally, non-traditional	
transfer	transferable, transferred, transferring	
trend		
underlie	underlay, *underlying*	
unique	uniquely, uniqueness	
utilize	utilization, *utility*	
vary	variability, variable, *variables*, variably, variance, variant, variation, varied, varying invariable, invariably	
vision		

Introduction

About the author

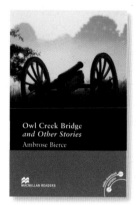

Owl Creek Bridge and *Beyond the Wall* are taken from *Owl Creek Bridge and Other Stories* by Ambrose Bierce, a title from the Macmillan Readers series.

Ambrose Gwinnett Bierce was an American journalist and writer. He was born in Meigs County, in the state of Ohio, on 24 June, 1842, but he grew up in the state of Indiana. When the American Civil War began, Bierce became an officer in the Union Army. He helped to make maps for the Unionists.

Bierce worked in Britain between 1872 and 1876. Then he returned to America, and went to San Francisco on the West Coast. He became the editor of the newspapers, the *San Francisco News-Letter* and the *California Advertiser*. He wrote reports about theatre plays and books.

Bierce admired the American writer, Edgar Allan Poe. He liked Poe's stories about ghosts, horror, and mystery. Many of Bierce's own stories were about strange mysteries and ghosts. But his stories about the American Civil War made him famous.

In 1913, when he was seventy-one, Ambrose Bierce went to Mexico. There was a war in Mexico at this time, and Bierce wrote newspaper reports about the fighting. Ambrose Bierce disappeared during a battle at Ojinaga, on 11 January, 1914. His body was never found.

The places in these stories

America during the Civil War 1861–1865

Owl Creek Bridge

A man stood on the edge of a railroad bridge in Alabama. His feet were on one end of a plank. Standing on the other end of this long flat piece of wood were two soldiers. An officer stood a few yards away from the soldiers and watched what was happening.

The man looked down at the Owl Creek River that flowed twenty feet below him. One end of a long rope was tied to the railroad bridge. The other end of the rope was tied around the man's neck. His hands were tied behind his back with a short cord.

The man turned and looked around him. A railroad track came out of a forest and ran across the wooden bridge to a small fort. The fort stood on the northern bank of the river. Soldiers with rifles guarded each end of the bridge.

All the soldiers wore blue uniforms. They were soldiers of the Union Army and they were a long way from their homes in the north.

The man with the rope around his neck was not far from his home. His name was Peyton Farquhar. Peyton's home and his family were on the other side of the forest. But Peyton was not going to see them again. He was going to be hanged. When the two soldiers stepped off the plank, one end of it would lift up and Peyton would fall. When he fell, the rope would break his neck.

It was sunrise on a summer day. The sun was coming up above the trees in the east. Peyton looked down at the river below him again. The water was deep. Could he break the cord and free his hands? Could he jump into the river, swim away, and escape?

Peyton was not a soldier, he was a rich landowner. He was thirty-five years old and he wore fine clothes. He was a well-educated gentleman. He had a handsome face, long hair and a dark beard and moustache. Members of Peyton's family had lived in the southern state of Alabama for a hundred years. Slaves worked on his plantation. Now the Union Army – the Yankees – had invaded the Confederate state of Alabama. Peyton was not a soldier in the Confederate Army. But he wanted to defend his home against the invaders from the north.

A man had visited Peyton's house two days earlier and he had given Peyton an idea. The man had been wearing a grey uniform. He had told Peyton that he was a Confederate scout. The scout watched where and when Yankee regiments moved and how many men there were. Then he reported this information to his commanding officer.

Peyton looked down at the river below him.

'We tried to stop the Yankees moving further into this state. We destroyed the railroad track,' the scout told Peyton. 'But they repaired the track. A group of Yankees have now reached the bridge over Owl Creek. There are only a few hundred Yankee soldiers at the creek now, but soon there will be many more. They'll come on trains.'

'How can we stop them?' asked Peyton.

'We need more of our own men,' said the soldier. 'More of our soldiers *are* coming. We can keep the Yankees at the river, but we need to delay them. We must keep them on the northern side of the bridge. Our men are not far away.'

'I know Owl Creek Bridge,' said Peyton. 'In winter, the rain carries tree branches down the river. Branches are trapped under the bridge now. I'll make a fire in the branches. They'll burn easily and so will the wooden bridge. I'll burn the bridge!'

'Be careful,' said the scout. 'If the Yankees catch you, they'll hang you.'

So Peyton had gone to Owl Creek Bridge before sunrise. He had moved quietly along the southern bank of the river, but the bridge was well-guarded. Union soldiers had caught Peyton before he burned the bridge. And now he stood on the edge of the bridge with a rope around his neck.

Peyton looked down at a piece of wood that floated on the surface of the water. The river was deep and the water was moving very fast. He looked up at the sky. The bright sun had now risen above the trees. The short rope that was tied around Peyton's hands was too strong. He could not break the cord and he could not untie it. Peyton closed his eyes and thought about his wife and children. He did not want to die.

The Yankee officer shouted an order. The soldiers stepped off the wooden plank and Peyton fell toward the river. He felt a sharp pain in his neck. Then he heard a loud noise – SNAP! The rope had broken! Peyton fell into the river and went down and down into the deep dark water.

As soon as the ropes were wet, they became loose. The cord around Peyton's hands was no longer tight. He pulled the cord from his hands, and the rope around his neck fell away. Peyton was a strong swimmer. Now his hands were free and he could swim up through the water. He kicked his legs and went up towards the surface.

Peyton opened his eyes and saw daylight. He was glad to be alive. He breathed deeply. He looked at the sky and the trees as if he was seeing them for the first time. The colours of the sky and the leaves on the trees were bright and strong.

Suddenly he heard loud voices. The soldiers were shouting as they looked down from the bridge. They were aiming their rifles down at the water.

Peyton heard the sound of a gun firing. Then he heard a bullet splash into the water and he saw a small cloud of smoke on the bridge. All the soldiers on the bridge were looking at him. They were aiming their rifles at him. One of the soldiers had fired his gun at Peyton. Peyton dived under the surface of the water and began to swim away from the bridge.

All the soldiers fired their rifles. It took them half a minute to reload their guns. But Peyton was not far enough away from the bridge. The soldiers could still shoot him before he reached a safer place! Peyton swam faster.

Suddenly he heard a loud whistling sound. The guards had fired the cannon that was in the small fort at the northern end of the bridge. There was a terrible noise as the cannon shell exploded. Boom! Pieces of the shell crashed into the trees on the bank of the river. The cannon fired again. Another shell crashed in the river near Peyton's head. He began to swim quickly towards the southern bank of the river. The soldiers on the bridge fired their rifles again.

Peyton reached the river bank. The water was shallow here. His feet touched the soft sand at the bottom of the river and he stood up. He ran out of the water, toward the trees. As he ran, he held his head low. At any moment, a bullet might hit his back. Peyton ran into the forest and hid behind a large tree for a few minutes. Was he safe?

The Yankee soldiers could not see Peyton now, but he knew that he must go further into the forest. The cannon fired again and another shell crashed through the trees. The soldiers shouted as they ran across the bridge and came into the trees. Peyton ran deeper into the forest.

A strange light shone through the trees. Peyton felt as if he was in a dream. The leaves of the trees shone like bright green jewels. The smell of the flowers was strong and sweet.

It was warm in the forest and Peyton was tired. He wanted to rest. He wanted to stay here forever. But he had to escape from the Yankees. He had to go home.

Peyton walked on and on. Was there no end to the forest? Peyton had lived near this forest all his life, but he did not recognize any of it. He did not know where he was. This was a wild, strange place.

The sun rose higher in the sky. Peyton was hungry and tired, but he thought about his home and his family. He must go home – he must see his wife and children. He had to walk south, so he walked with the sun on his right side.

He walked all day. He walked until the sun set and night fell.

At last he came to a path in the forest. The path was as straight as a city street. The tall trees on both sides of the path were like black walls. They went straight ahead like the lines on the plan of a building. When Peyton looked up, he saw bright stars in the dark sky. But he did not recognize them. They did not look like the stars that he remembered. He heard voices whispering in the forest. The trees were talking in a language that he did not understand.

Peyton was very hot and very tired. He was thirsty too, but he did not stop to find water. He walked along the straight path. He was not far from his home.

On and on he walked. He was half-asleep and half-awake. The danger and excitement on the bridge had made Peyton extremely tired. His neck was very painful but he walked on. He knew that his house was near. It was at the end of the path. He was almost home. He was almost safe. Here the ground was soft. He no longer felt his feet moving on the soft grass. He forgot his hunger and thirst and pain.

Suddenly it is daylight and Peyton is standing in front of his own home. He must have travelled all through the night. He pushes open his garden gate. His sweet wife is waiting for him on the steps of his house. She is smiling. How beautiful she is! Everything is bright and beautiful in the morning sunshine. Everything looks the same, but it is also brighter and clearer. Peyton has come home. But as he puts his arms around his wife he feels a sudden, terrible pain in his neck. A white light shines brightly. Then there is darkness and silence.

Peyton Farquhar was dead. His neck was broken. His body hung from the rope under Owl Creek Bridge.

Beyond the Wall

was born in the United States, but I lived in Hong Kong for many years. My business in Asia was successful and I became rich. After twenty years, I decided to visit my home in New York. On my way from Hong Kong to New York, I stayed one week in California.

I had a friend who lived in the city of San Francisco and I wanted to see him again. His name was Mohun Dampier and he had been my friend for many years. We had written many letters to each other. But recently, I had not received any news from him.

Dampier had never had a job. His father gave him a little money, so Dampier had never worked.

Dampier was a superstitious man. He believed that luck or magic could make things happen in his life. He spent most of his time reading books – strange books. Most of the books were about occult philosophy. I called them books about magic.

As soon as I arrived in San Francisco, I sent a message to Dampier's house. The message said: *I am staying in San Francisco for three days. May I visit you?*

Dampier surprised me. An hour later, he sent a servant to my hotel with a reply.

Come to my house at once, my dear friend, he wrote. *Come this evening. You'll remember the house – I'm sure. It was my father's home. I live in a tower at one end of the house. You don't have to ring the bell or knock on the door. I'll tell the servants to go to bed. And I'll leave the front door of the tower open. Come up the stairs immediately. I'll be waiting for you. Please come soon.*

I rode in a cab to Dampier's house. That evening, the weather was stormy. A strong wind was blowing and cold rain was falling. I had forgotten that California is cold and wet in winter. I only remembered the sunshine, not the wind and the rain.

Dampier's house was near the Pacific Ocean. It was an ugly, two-story building that was made of bricks. There was a tower at one end. The house was surrounded by a garden of many trees and beautiful plants. But now it was winter and there were no leaves on the trees or flowers on the plants.

The driver stopped his cab near the tower. Although the front door was only five yards away, I became soaked with rain as soon as I stepped out of the cab. I ran to the door of the tower and turned the handle.

The door was unlocked and I opened it. One small lamp burned on the stairway and it did not give much light. The hall was full of shadows and I could not see clearly. I climbed the stairs slowly, touching the wall with my fingers. At the top of the stairs there was another door. I opened it and went into a room that was lit with another small lamp.

Dampier came forwards, held my hand and shook it. He was wearing a long silk coat and soft leather slippers on his feet. His clothes were old-fashioned and strange.

We looked at each other and I was shocked. I had not seen Dampier for many years. My friend had changed a lot! He had been a handsome man, but now his hair was grey and his face was very pale. There were many lines around his eyes and mouth. Dampier looked like a thin old man, but he was not older than fifty. His large and bright eyes shone strangely in the shadowy room.

'Welcome, my friend! Please sit down,' he said.

Dampier offered me some wine and a cigar and we talked a little. But I am afraid that our conversation was not very interesting. Meeting friends after many years can be difficult and it can make you sad. Maybe Dampier guessed my thoughts.

'*Non sum qualis eram* – I'm not as I was,' he said.

I tried to make a joke. 'Your Latin hasn't improved,' I replied.

My friend smiled. 'Latin is a dead language and I'm a dead man,' he said. Then his smile disappeared and he said, 'I'll die very soon.'

I did not know what to say. I smoked my cigar and drank my wine. We were both silent for several minutes. Outside, the wind had stopped blowing. I wanted to leave the house.

Suddenly I heard a strange noise. TAP. TAP. TAP. It was the sound of someone, or something, knocking. Was the sound coming from one wall of the tower? TAP. TAP. TAP. The sound was not quick or loud. It was not the sound of someone knocking loudly on a door. The soft tapping sounded like someone sending a signal – a message.

Dampier had forgotten me. He was staring at the wall. There was a strange expression on his face. My friend looked excited and afraid. His eyes shone brightly.

I did not know what to do. Should I go or stay? I stood up.

'I – I see that you are very tired,' I said. 'I'll leave. May I visit you tomorrow?'

Dampier turned his head and looked at me.

'Please stay,' he said. 'There's no problem. Nobody is there.'

He walked to a small window and opened it. I had not noticed the window earlier.

'Look,' he said.

I walked across the room and looked out of the window.

I could see nothing except the light of a street lamp and rain falling. No one was standing outside. There was no one near the wall of the tower.

'Please don't leave me,' said Dampier. 'I must tell you a story. You're the only man that I can tell it to. Will you listen to my story?'

I wanted to go back to my hotel. Dampier, his house, and the strange noise made me feel uncomfortable. I think that I am a sensible and intelligent man. But I felt unhappy and frightened in that old tower room. However, I did not want to upset my old friend.

'Very well,' I said. 'I'll stay and listen.'

Dampier poured me another drink and offered me another cigar. Then he began to tell his story.

'I didn't move into this house until my father died,' Dampier said. 'That was ten years ago, when I was about forty years old. When my father died, I got his business, his property, and his money.

Before his death, I lived in a large apartment building on Rincon Hill,' said Dampier. 'Maybe you know that area of San Francisco? Rincon Hill was a fashionable area fifty years ago, but now it is run-down and neglected. The owner of the apartment building rented out many of its small rooms. The walls of the rooms were thin. You could almost put your hand through them.

I was lucky,' Dampier went on. 'The rent was cheap and I had a large room in the building. No one visited me. And no one disturbed me – I could study my books quietly. I lived happily on Rincon Hill.

One morning, as I was leaving the apartment, I saw a young girl,' Dampier continued. 'It was a warm day in June. She was wearing a white dress and a straw hat. There were brightly-coloured flowers and ribbons around the brim of the hat. Then I saw the girl's face. It's difficult to find words to describe it. Her face was strange and beautiful. I had never seen such a beautiful face before. Without thinking, I lifted my hat and bowed. She looked at me with shining brown eyes, but she didn't speak. I knew that she was pleased to see me, but she didn't smile. She went into the house and shut the door. I stood and stared at the closed door. Would I see her again? Should I speak to her? Would *she* speak to *me*?

Maybe you think that these are the thoughts of a much younger man,' said Dampier. 'And maybe you're right. But these feelings were new to me. I'd never been in love before. I'd spent too many years with books and too little time with people. Now I believe that you're my only friend. Soon, none of this will matter. I don't feel foolish when I talk to you.'

Dampier stopped speaking for a few moments, then he went on with his story.

'The next day, I waited in my apartment. For many hours, I stared out of the window. I watched the street, but the girl didn't come out of the building. I didn't know her name, so I couldn't ask anyone about her. That night I couldn't sleep. The next morning, I sat by the window again and waited.

Then suddenly, she came out of the apartment building and I went out, too. But when I reached the street, she had disappeared. I didn't see where she had gone, so I walked around the neighbourhood. At last I saw her in a narrow street. We smiled at each other. She recognized me, I'm sure of that. From that time, I often went out when the girl went out. She always wore the straw hat with the brightly-coloured flowers and ribbons on its brim. I didn't follow her. I simply walked around the neighborhood, and hoped to see her again.

At last, I went to the landlady of the apartment. "Who is the girl with the pretty face and the straw hat?" I asked her. "She's my niece, sir," the landlady replied. "She's a servant in this house. She lives here because her parents are dead. She works for me – she cooks and cleans the building. I also send her to buy our food. She lives at the top of the house. Her room is next to yours, but at the top of the other staircase."

Oh, my friend! I wish that I'd never heard that piece of information,' Dampier said to me. 'The girl's room was next to mine. She was on the other side of the thin wall. At night, I put my hand on the wall and I thought of her. Was her bed by the wall? Was she sleeping only a few inches from my hand?

I couldn't study because of the girl,' said Dampier. 'My mind wasn't clear. I only thought about the girl. I couldn't study my books about the occult.

I'd never wanted to marry,' Dampier went on. 'I'd never wanted a wife and children. I was only interested in learning. And I could never marry a poor, uneducated servant girl. My father would never have given his permission. All my money came from my father. If he had stopped giving me money… well…'

'What happened next?' I asked.

My friend looked at me sadly.

'I stopped waiting for her and I stopped watching her. I only studied. I spent all my time reading my books. But one hot night I couldn't sleep. Thoughts were racing round and round in my mind. I thought again and again about the beautiful girl. I wanted to be with her. She was only on the other side of the wall! I tapped on the wall. I tapped very gently three times. TAP. TAP. TAP. I tapped again. TAP. TAP. TAP. Then I felt foolish. I was behaving like a boy who is in love for the first time. I got out of my bed and began to study my books.

I was reading a strange book,' Dampier said. 'It was a book of occult philosophy by Necromantius. You would call it a book of magic and superstition. In his book, Necromantius describes how to be a fortune-teller. Necromantius also wrote about strange and terrible things that happen three times. When these things happened three times, death would come. Necromantius called this a "fatal triad". I believe that a fatal triad has happened to me.'

'Why?' I asked. 'What happened?'

'While I was alone, reading that strange book by Necromantius,' said Dampier, 'I heard a sound. It was a soft tapping sound. It came from beyond the wall. It was the answer to my own signal! TAP. TAP. TAP. I knew that the pretty servant girl was sending a message to me. She wanted me to come to her. I ran to the wall and tapped my signal again. TAP. TAP. TAP. But after that, there was silence. She didn't reply to any of my other signals. I listened for many hours, but I heard nothing more.

For many days after this, I looked for the girl,' Dampier said. 'But I never saw her again. I tried to forget her. Then one evening, I went to bed early because I was very tired. In the middle of the night, I awoke suddenly. I had heard a soft sound. I opened my eyes and sat up. I heard a soft tapping on the wall beside the bed. In a few moments, it was repeated. TAP. TAP. TAP. I was going to reply to the signal, then I stopped. The girl hadn't replied to my last messages. I would *not* reply to *her* now!'

Dampier drank a little wine and then continued.

'I lay in the bed listening,' he said. 'But I didn't reply. At last, I must have slept. When I woke, it was late and I felt tired. I needed some fresh air, so I went out of my apartment. The landlady was outside my door. "Oh, Mr Dampier," she said. "Have you heard the terrible news?"

'My heart began to beat quickly. My voice shook when I answered. "W–what news?" I asked her. "My poor niece was sick

"'I ran to the wall and tapped my signal again.'"

for a week," the landlady replied. "Didn't you know? I've seen you watching her. Didn't you know that she was ill?"

I was shocked,' said Dampier. 'I didn't know what to say. Yes. I *had* looked at the girl, but I'd never spoken to her. My mind was always full of thoughts of my books and thoughts of her. How much time had passed since I had seen the girl? A few days? A week? I couldn't remember.

"And how is your niece now?" I asked the landlady. "I'm sorry, sir," the landlady replied. '"he was very ill last night and I took care of her. The poor girl made only one request. She wanted her bed to be moved. She wanted her bed to be beside the wall – the wall next to your room. So we moved her bed. This made her feel happier, poor thing. Then she touched the wall and smiled. A few hours later, she died." '

The expression on Dampier's face was terrible. There were tears in his eyes as he continued his story.

'When I heard this news, I nearly died too,' said my friend. 'I didn't know what to say. What had I done? I had sent my thoughts to the girl and she had answered. I had not called out in words. I had used occult philosophy – magic – to send her a message.'

Dampier was silent for a few minutes. Then he went on.

'A few days later, I heard of my father's death,' said Dampier sadly. 'I left the apartment on Rincon Hill and came to his house – this house. It's been my home since then. I've been waiting here, in this tower, for ten years. I've been waiting for a visitor. I wasn't expecting to see you, but your visit wasn't a surprise. Necromantius tells us how signs are repeated three times. You've heard my story. You must decide if my story has happened because of a fatal triad. I heard the tapping twice before. The first time, I tried to find the person who made the noise. The second time, many signals were sent to me but I didn't reply. Now you've heard the tapping, too. That was the third time. The fatal triad is complete.'

I stood up and shook Dampier's hand. My friend knew that I understood his sadness and pain. He pressed my hand with his fingers and smiled. I said goodnight. There was nothing more to say.

The next morning, a servant came from Dampier's house. He brought a sad message for me. My friend, Mohun Dampier, had died in the night.